SECRETS OF NEXT LEVEL ENTREPRENEURS

SECRETS OF
NEXT LEVEL
ENTREPRENEURS

11 Powerful Lessons to Thrive in Business and Lead a Balanced Life

ALEX BRUECKMANN

WITH CONTRIBUTIONS BY

Dr. Hermann Simon * Teresa Quinlan * Tony Martignetti
Charlene Li * Sheetal Khullar * Dr. Ken Keis
Dr. Terry Jackson * Angela Howard * Jerry Fu, PharmD

WILEY

For general information on our other products and services or for technical support, please contact our Customer Care Department within the United States at (800) 762-2974, outside the United States at (317) 572-3993 or fax (317) 572-4002.

Wiley also publishes its books in a variety of electronic formats. Some content that appears in print may not be available in electronic formats. For more information about Wiley products, visit our web site at www.wiley.com.

Library of Congress Cataloging-in-Publication Data is Available:

ISBN: 9781394185382 (cloth)
ISBN: 9781394185399 (ePub)
ISBN: 9781394185405 (ePDF)

COVER DESIGN: COURTESY OF THE AUTHOR

SKY10042382_020223

Contents

Introduction
Why I Compiled This Book and Who It Is For

We have gotten used to reading that we live in unprecedented times, that the speed of change and disruption has never been greater than now, and that our world is increasingly volatile, uncertain, complex, and ambiguous. As if we had required any more proof that these statements are true, the COVID-19 pandemic and the war in Ukraine remind us that peace, prosperity, and health cannot be taken for granted. Effectively, we are witnessing supply chain disruptions and inflation rates higher than we've seen in recent decades, especially in the Western hemisphere.

We have been adjusting our consumption patterns, with consequences for how much money we spend. We see new demands from an increasingly flexible workforce, challenging traditional career paths and prioritizing their personal over work lives. Digital innovation has maintained a high pace. While it enables new business models and entire industries on the positive end, it can also feel overwhelming to keep up to speed with digital transformation.

Countless businesses, small and large, were swept away by the chain of events that sparked in 2020. Some of them had operated unsustainably for a while; for them, these crises were the nail in the coffin. Others operated under business models that were profitable but too inflexible. They got dragged under the bus because they couldn't adjust to a rapidly changing environment. All other businesses must learn the lessons and equip themselves for the next inevitable inflection point. And come it will.

If we learned one takeaway over the past two decades, it is hopefully this: the next crisis is already waiting around the corner. I have spent almost my entire adult life in one crisis or another, from the dot-com bubble burst, the war on terrorism, the financial crisis, the state debt crisis, the refugee crisis, the COVID-19 pandemic, and Russia's war in Ukraine, to name the most prominent ones.

Let's be honest: crisis mode seems to be the new normal. And most of these crises are outside our immediate circle of control. But it's not all doom and gloom. The changing landscape opens opportunities for business owners willing to create more appealing offerings for consumers, employees, and shareholders. Instead of hoping and waiting for better times, we must adjust our businesses strategically and operationally to make the most out of what we can immediately influence.

As entrepreneurs, corporate leaders, and business owners, we must prepare ourselves and those who work with us for the future. It starts with us and how we grow beyond what we know today. What made us successful in the first place—the subject matter expertise we used to build our businesses—will not suffice to create the same caliber of success. We must learn essential skills, understand ourselves, and shift our mindsets accordingly. The time is now to reach the next level and grow beyond existing limits—personally and professionally.

There are three mission-critical pillars that contribute to building future-proof businesses: strategy, leadership, and self-care. It's essential to strategically re-adjust a business for success, consciously shape leadership and culture, and practice self-care as we humbly accept our limitations as entrepreneurs and leaders.

Instead of celebrating the hustle culture, promoting a glamorous view of entrepreneurship, or glorifying the few that amassed incredible wealth, this book is about, what I call, *Next-Level Entrepreneurship*. It's about building businesses that take the right steps to do well, be profitable, and contribute to building more equitable communities. It is for entrepreneurs and leaders who embrace their responsibility for social and environmental justice, and are eager to contribute to a world worth living in—for us, our children, and generations to come.

This book holds specific advice on issues that are on the mind of every business owner and leader at one point or another. I invited some of the brightest minds to contribute their perspectives on Next-Level Entrepreneurship. We shed light on a range of interconnected topics that are critical success factors in today's business world. This is not a theoretical textbook. Instead, we offer actionable solutions that you can put into practice right away—written *by* business owners and leaders *for* business owners and leaders.

Based on his ten commandments, Hermann Simon helps us sharpen our understanding of pricing in a high inflation environment. With the zeitgeist shifting our perception of businesses, Sheetal Khullar introduces a model for a socially and environmentally sustainable business approach. Tony Martignetti and Terry Jackson offer insights into leadership components that allow us to build people-centric, high-performance cultures in the workplace. Teresa Quinlan and Ken Keis show ways to overcome the outdated paradigm of work-life balance and instead self-actualize and achieve personal transformation.

Depending on your personal experience, some chapters will be easier to engage with—previously overlooked perspectives are waiting for you as you read some chapters with a beginner's mind. Other chapters hold suggestions that might feel unfamiliar or foreign at first sight. Allow yourself to approach them with the open mind of an eager learner to explore what's in it for you.

I encourage you to embrace the full variety of topics we cover, as all of them are critical factors to living a happier, healthier, and more fulfilling life—including leading a limitless business.

You'll find that each chapter comes with an 'About the Author' section. Many of the authors have published books on their subjects that will help you dive deep into your topics of interest. The authors invite you to connect on social media and to benefit from additional resources on their websites.

With that, I hope you enjoy the book and stay courageous.

1

Three Essential Hard Skills Every Business Leader Should Master

The first theme addresses some essential hard skills for business leaders. I chose three topics that I consider highly relevant for anyone leading a company. In my over twenty years of working in business, I've collaborated with many types of entrepreneurs and corporate leaders. They range from early-stage start-ups to solopreneurs. Others are leaders of medium-sized enterprises, some of them family-owned, and others are corporate leaders of global enterprises.

While these managers have varying needs in many ways, they do have more than a few things in common:

- they all operate in a marketplace with competitors
- all of them want to sell their offerings to clients
- they are all affected by consumer demands for a more sustainable way of doing business

No matter the size of a business, its industry, or governance structure, these three topics have major implications for any business leader.

First, leaders need to understand strategy as a discipline to be able to paint a compelling vision for their business and create a strategy to bring their vision to life. Every business leader and entrepreneur needs to develop a level of strategic understanding sufficient enough to lead the way. Without a strategic plan in place, businesses lack clarity and direction. As a consequence, companies allocate resources to priorities that aren't mission-critical whatsoever. The resulting lack of focus leads businesses to stretch themselves too thin and miss out on what really matters for success. In my first chapter, I will focus on the topic of business strategy, using the examples of go-to-market strategies for start-ups and competitive strategies for corporations. The key to mastering business strategy is a consistent definition of 'strategy,' a thorough understanding of the significant characteristics for an impactful strategy, and the place that ethics holds in strategy.

The second implication is that business leaders need a better understanding of the biggest lever of profitability: pricing their services and products accurately. Especially during times of high inflation, pricing plays a crucial role in protecting your bottom line. Dr. Hermann Simon, world-renowned management thinker and leading pricing authority, shares actionable insights on how to maximize the profit potential through pricing. He describes easy-to-implement approaches to discover the essential pricing drivers for your offering and how to turn them into measurable results. He also shares his ten commandments for pricing in times of inflation, which come in handy. Simon describes the benefits of value-pricing and why you should focus on economic profit as the ultimate measure of profitability.

Once we understand how to implement tailored strategy and pricing to our business, we can move on to the third implication for leaders: we need to better understand how to realign our businesses sustainably. Companies embracing their responsibility to impact this world positively can strongly benefit from changing market demands, fueled by more conscious consumption patterns. Reshaping a business's role by contributing to social and environmental justice is about combining planet, people, and profits into one cohesive approach. Sheetal Khullar, a sustainable development and impact strategist, shares how we can overcome skepticism when talking about sustainability and profits. She shows us how businesses can fill knowledge gaps, create new value-based consumer touchpoints, and build effective partnerships.

1

Creating a Winning Business Strategy—It's Easier Said Than Done

Alex Brueckmann

If you ask three business owners "what is strategy?" you will likely receive three different definitions. Their answers might range from "a plan on how we create value" or "our priorities for the next few years" to "an approach to winning against competitors" and "a framework used to make decisions." There is nothing wrong with these answers. As a matter of fact, if you research a definition of the term strategy, you will find suggestions that match these ideas to a large degree. So, which definition is the most accurate? Which approach should be used for your business?

I would accept any definition of strategy as long as it captures some of these ideas if used consistently in your business. This can prevent businesses from running into major issues with severe consequences. The term strategy is highly versatile in all aspects of life, from the world of sports to business and beyond. It does not come as a surprise that many find it difficult to make sense of it.

This chapter will focus on strategy using examples of go-to-market strategies for start-ups and competitive strategies for corporations. I will define what strategy is, describe the characteristics and importance of an impactful strategy, and examine the ethics of strategy.

What Is a Strategy Anyway?

The first matter to take care of is to define the term itself. For start-ups and entrepreneurs, the term strategy is closely associated with go-to-market strategy: how they plan to penetrate a specific market with a new product, technology, or service offering. Serial entrepreneur Richard Branson, the founder of Virgin Group, is quoted to have said, "And in the end, you just got to say, 'Screw it, just do it' and get on and try it."[1] Now, Branson certainly made some significant business decisions in his life, and some questionable ones as well. Having learned from observing

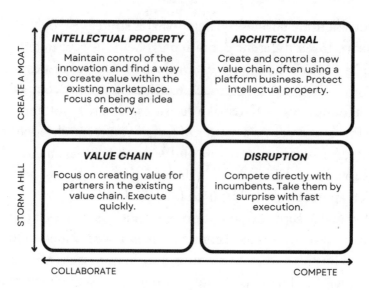

FIGURE 1.1 The Entrepreneurial Strategy Compass, adapted from Joshua Gans, et al.[2]

Branson, let me suggest that a 'screw it, just do it' attitude is the opposite of having a strategy at play. You might want to approach your business with a more focused approach.

A simple way to develop a straightforward strategy is to start with the Entrepreneurial Strategy Compass. It describes four types of strategies that help founders and entrepreneurs make educated, rather than impulsive, go-to-market decisions.

How would these strategic go-to-market options look in operation for a real business? To understand further, I've come up with a not-so-hypothetical scenario. Let's assume you are an aspiring entrepreneur living in Bellevue, Washington, USA. It is 1994, your name is Jeffrey, and you want to launch a business based on your best idea: selling books online. You examine the following strategic options to consider your ideal strategy to enter the market:

Option 1: Disruption—you pick one product category, books, and move fast. You compete against giant book retailers and take them by surprise. They don't take you seriously at first; however, your mission is to change that.

Option 2: Architectural—you create and control a new platform and allow retailers to sell their products via Amazon.

Option 3: Value Chain—you partner with publishing houses, helping them circumvent retailers as gatekeepers and use Amazon as the key to a profitable business-to-consumer (B2C) business.

Option 4: Intellectual Property—you help large retailers modernize their sales channels and build a white-label online bookstore.

Strategic Specificity Matters More Than You Might Think

It seems that Jeff Bezos maneuvered his strategic options wisely. Now, Amazon can hardly be described as a start-up anymore, but rather a significant corporate player. In the corporate world, the term strategy describes an organization's business or competitive strategy. There are many examples of how the term lacks specificity—and the potential issues that arise. Let me share two particularly notable examples, which are publicly accessible on the respective company websites of Porsche and Boeing.

Example 1: Porsche—2025 Strategy

"The company's main objective is to achieve value-generating growth. Only by achieving such growth can we make sustainable investments in innovative technologies, new products, and, most importantly, in our team here at Porsche. With this approach, we are already on our way toward rethinking sporty mobility. We want to excite customers with our products and services. We also aim to consolidate our reputation as an excellent employer and business partner that fulfills its social and environmental responsibilities. And the return needs to be sufficient too."

Porsche's strategy consists of four key pillars:

1. Excellent employer and business partner
2. Inspiring customers with a unique product and brand experience
3. Excellent profitability with a return on sales of more than 15 percent
4. Innovation and sustainable business practices.[3]

The pillars are specific, immediately showing an understanding of their intentions and direction. Porsche's four pillars are linked to each other; they also are mutually beneficial and could not stand on their own. No pillar is self-sustaining, and each point contributes to the main objective of value-generating growth. Also, the pillars align with their company: anyone reading them can quickly develop a clear understanding of any of them.

This is a solid explanation of Porsche's main priorities and focus. It consists of concise sentences, is clearly structured, and contains a timeframe with ways to measure their success. Let's be clear: this strategy description is better than many other examples of company business strategies.

Example 2: Boeing—2025 Strategy

"Enterprise Strategy:

- *Operate as One Boeing*
- *Build Strength on Strength*
- *Sharpen and Accelerate to Win*

  2025 Goals:

- *Market Leadership*
- *Top-quartile Performance and Returns*

- *Growth Fueled by Productivity*
- *Design, Manufacturing, Services Excellence*
- *Accelerated Innovation*
- *Global Scale and Depth*
- *Best Team, Talent and Leaders*
- *Top Corporate Citizen"* [4]

Let's briefly examine the Boeing strategy. It does not consist of proper sentences and lists three brief bullet points, followed by eight goals for 2025. This hardly qualifies as a strategy. It's a nondescript list rather than a description anyone can read and comprehend. The three main bullet points couldn't be more generic and resemble internal corporate marketing jargon.

The parts that could be measurable are unspecific. For example, it's unclear what they mean by "Top-quartile," as it could refer to Fortune 500 companies, airplane producers, the aviation industry, or any number of things. The content and direction of the three strategic themes leave maximum room for interpretation, as they are nonspecific and very short. In addition, it is unclear how Boeing's themes and goals are related.

Since the 1970s, Boeing's business strategies have resulted in a creeping loss of market share to its primary rival, Airbus. In the 2000s, Boeing failed to develop more fuel-efficient passenger planes. It became a major problem when their competitor Airbus, introduced the A320neo, which became a best-seller. Boeing didn't have a comparable aircraft ready to compete. Due to the time and cost involved in designing a new plane from scratch, Boeing decided to update their existing 737 model with larger and more fuel-efficient engines and related design additions, sold as the 737 MAX. An upgrade.

In October 2018, and again in March 2019, two 737 MAX aircraft crashed, with 346 casualties. The fallout for Boeing was significant. The 737 MAX models lost their clearance and were grounded. A United States Federal Aviation Agency investigation revealed that design flaws concealed by Boeing caused the disasters. As a result, the company lost the trust of regulators and the public. The total direct costs of the 737 MAX groundings are an estimated US$20 billion, and indirect costs are over US$60 billion. This excludes the US$2.5 billion settlement Boeing paid after being charged with fraud to avoid criminal prosecution.[5] While I'm not suggesting that it was only because of their strategy—culture and leadership appear to have played a role as well—Boeing paid a high toll for their mistakes.

I chose to examine Boeing's and Porsche's public plans to illustrate how vastly different strategies can look, and how various companies communicate their strategies to the public. I'm sure internally, both companies adopt a more succinct and focused version of their strategies. However, this is what Boeing and Porsche are publicly declaring and sharing as their strategy.

Other companies publish strategies that are looser vision statements, aspirations, or missions, which hardly qualify as strategies. Almost every organization I have worked with started by creating a new strategy based on an unclear understanding of the term strategy. But all of them—despite the fuzziness—still used the term, in one way or another, despite their varying directions. For example:

> 'We need a new pricing strategy to compete with the other players in the market.'
>
> 'Our hiring strategy is not delivering the talent pipeline we expect.'
>
> 'We need a clear strategy for the purchasing discussion next week.'
>
> 'Our digital product strategy is outdated.'

This omnipresent yet blurry understanding of the term 'strategy' tends to cause even more issues up to the very top of organizations within senior leadership teams.

Define The Term 'Strategy' for Your Business

Ideally, a leadership team typically consists of accomplished professionals with years of experience. In these years, they would have seen different strategies, some more successfully implemented than others. They would have had exciting and sometimes long and tiring discussions about strategy. They would have potentially read classic books, such as *Competitive Strategy* by Michael E. Porter, who defines strategy as *"a competitive position, deliberately choosing a different set of activities to deliver a unique mix of value"*.[6] And now these very individuals embark on a business venture to define a new strategy based on the variety of experiences and preconceived notions about what a strategy is, and what it should contain, in their views.

As a result of this misalignment, discussions about strategy are difficult and must be interpreted on a case-by-case basis, with their thoughts and individual understanding. Over time, my colleagues and I understood that before we could start strategizing with a client, we needed to help those involved form a common understanding of what 'strategy' meant and how they would use the term going forward. What we often achieved was a common understanding and a definition along these lines:

> "A strategy is a framework against which we make decisions to sustainably deliver our unique value to our customers, employees, and suppliers. It is a plan describing how we win in our chosen marketplace, where the unique value of our offering is repeatedly chosen over our competitor's offering."

Based on this definition, let's describe what strategy is—and what strategy is *not*.

What strategy is	What strategy is *not*
A set of key priorities to achieve a desired vision or goal, (i.e., a desired state in the future)	A rigid and detailed plan that doesn't change
A plan that captures how you create value for employees, suppliers, and customers	A magical formula that guarantees future business success
A way to achieve results that will make your customers go "wow!" and leave your competition baffled, asking, "how did they do that?"	A formulated answer to questions of all disciplines in your company
A framework against which business decisions are made	A plan coping with every aspect of your business over the coming ten years
A guide to the next two to five years	Tactics
The big picture	A bold statement about the future
A map helping you maneuver the business through partly unchartered territory	

Without a Purposeful Strategy Businesses Can Quickly Derail

In the late 00s, I got to know an industry that was, and still is, heavily under pressure: high-volume printing. Back then, it involved mail-order catalogs, magazines, and direct mail. The company I worked for had a history of great financial success—and this success became their own worst enemy. For years, leadership and personnel alike had been clinging to the glorious past, where everyone had their share of the golden times. The issue was that these times were over, and the corporate culture had become complacent and change-averse. They were staying the course and hoping that better times would return; it seemed to be the 'strategy' for many.

With media advancements opening opportunities for e-commerce and publishers, market demand for catalogs and magazines had been shrinking rapidly. None of the leaders in the organization had experienced anything like this before in their careers. Until this point, change had occurred in small doses, within the subject expertise of those in charge; change used to be incremental. In the 00s, the pace of change had shifted towards rapid transformational change in the printing industry. With one eye on the past, and without a business strategy in place, leadership seemed paralyzed.

Having reaped the fruits for decades without a real need for strategy, shareholders now demanded fast and bold moves to turn this printing company around and stop the financial bleeding. They opened the playing field for a newly appointed CEO and a company restructuring. Supported by a major management consultancy, the company now developed a strategy—they gave it their all, but unfortunately, it was too little, too late. The company had missed the right time to design a future-proof strategy. The inevitable happened: shareholders lost their patience, the company was restructured, and thousands lost their jobs.

This example is a devastating testimony of failure. Certainly not the leadership legacy anyone wants to leave behind. If you are socially conscious, you must act before it is too late. The good news is that there are many examples of great businesses that aren't complacent. And there are examples of great entrepreneurs and leaders, perhaps someone like you. If you care about the future of your family, you will figure out the best way to provide for them. If you care about the future of the environment, you will find ways to reduce your carbon footprint. And if you care about the future of the community you live in, you will dedicate your spare time to work towards a great place to live. Unfortunately, care is not always a driver in business, and I am not suggesting that every business strategy has a noble or altruistic nature.

By looking around, you will quickly identify organizations with doubtful strategies. As a result, those organizations will lose a sense of their own identity. Over time, this process can hollow out the heart of an organization and profoundly damage the culture.

An organization that suffered this fate was American bank Wells Fargo & Company. Since 2011, the bank had artificially inflated its sales growth by creating over two million fake bank accounts and credit card activations. In 2016, after this so-called 'sandbagging scandal' had blown up, Wells Fargo paid a $185 million fine. The fine could be seen as pennies for a bank that size. The real fallout—apart from a loss of shareholder value—is more likely decreased trust by consumers, regulatory bodies, and investors. Not to mention the negative press worldwide and the public humiliation of former Wells Fargo CEO John Stumpf. In the aftermath, more than 5,000 employees were fired for misconduct, and in return, the bank sued its top management. In 2020, the US government banned John Stumpf from ever working at a bank again and issued him a $17.5 million fine.[7] This is just one example of what a derailed strategy without purpose can lead to. Unfortunately, there are more examples out there; just think back to what caused the banking crisis in 2008 and how the shock waves of this event affected the global economy and nations over more than a decade.

Having No Strategy in Place Is Unethical

There are exceptional organizations that combine strategy and purpose into something impactful, providing meaning and direction to employees, suppliers, customers, and shareholders. To avoid falling into the marketing trap of fancy purpose statements without anchoring, purpose needs a strategy. And vice versa. One cannot exist without the other. The purpose is why an organization exists and needs to be more than just platitudes. Your purpose legitimizes your business, accrediting you in the eyes of others, and goes way beyond making money or securing jobs. To borrow an expression from Steve Jobs, the purpose is the 'ding' you leave in the universe, which hopefully makes the world a better place.

Without purpose, strategy can quickly derail and become mainly about profit maximization. Famous examples of derailed strategies of the recent past include car manufacturers, banks, and major sports organizations. And purpose without strategy? Well, at least it includes good intentions, and you might even live up to it to a certain degree. But that would be little more than sheer luck and certainly not sustainable on a long-term scale.

Strategy without purpose becomes mainly about profit maximization.

Purpose without strategy is little more than just good intention.

Having no strategy in place is irresponsible and unethical.

As business owners, we carry responsibilities for our families, employees, and the communities we serve. If we run businesses unintentionally, without clarity about goals, and desired impact, we are irresponsible, even unethical, because we fail to live up to our responsibilities.

Without a clear strategy, businesses can lose everything at the snap of a finger: market value, the security of people's jobs, and the trust of business partners, clients, and the public.

Creating and implementing a purposeful strategy is about taking charge and shaping the future; it is about conscious decisions, with a clear focus. Without direction, you might as well jump on a random train leaving the station and hope for the best.

This was how shareholders and leadership of the printing company I worked for seemed to have steered the organization for many years. Eventually, their destination was shutting down facilities, sending thousands of people and their families into unemployment and angst. Having no strategy in place is irresponsible and unethical. It's like gambling with borrowed money and the jobs of those working for you. In the end, the casino bank wins, and everyone else loses.

For a moment, imagine if the leadership had put in place a proper strategy when the time was right, while the company was still enjoying the good times. Imagine they had backed up that strategy with a meaningful purpose that connected emotionally with the workforce. It seems likely that instead of just maximizing profits for as long as they could, the company could have established real value beyond money for their employees and the communities around them. Purpose is an essential element of organizational identity, it shapes the type of culture we envision, and lays a foundation for steering an organization through times of change. If leaders truly embrace their responsibility, they create space for their organizations to design strategies beyond money, beyond simply managing to maintain the status quo.

A Great Strategy Is Built on Reinforcing Loops

To describe the underlying behavioral patterns, Peter Senge, an American systems scientist, author, and senior lecturer at MIT Sloan School of Management, introduced the Circles of Causality: balancing loops and reinforcing loops.[8] A balancing loop starts when we realize a change, a problem, or a threat to the status quo. As a result, we panic, and react in ways to get rid of the problem. Once we've achieved that, we relax and enjoy the regained balance until the next threat occurs, and the cycle starts anew, because we forget to redesign our action patterns and the way we operate systemically. Just like a company that realizes that their business is suffering: they react by creating some sort of strategy, probably containing a push for more sales and a cost-cutting program. Once the company sees the results of these measures (i.e., an improved financial situation), they will maintain the new equilibrium until the pressure returns. It is a reactive, fear-based, and crisis-oriented approach resulting in strategies aiming to regain balance. And as they say, fear has never been a good advisor.

The second circle Senge describes is a growth cycle, unleashing energy: a reinforcing loop. It describes processes that reinforce the desired direction, so-called virtuous cycles, like feeling better after exercising, and therefore exercising more, then feeling better and better over time. A reinforcing loop could start with a purpose or vision, as opposed to a threat or issue, and stokes passion instead of fear. The subsequent action, as opposed to reaction, is future-oriented and aims to create new normals instead of regaining balance. This is why strategies need to be anchored in purpose, not in a problem. Great strategies create growth and new normals. And great leaders realize that the challenges they face today can only be matched by creating purposeful, impact-driven strategies that lead to virtuous cycles.

Future-proof strategies provide answers to the most burning frequently asked questions of the industry you are in, the company you represent, and the people you lead. They unite your people and unleash creativity and ownership, which are essential to tackling the challenges ahead. That is what ethical, purposeful, and conscious leaders do to secure the future for those they lead and serve. This is true wherever you sit in your organization, be it somewhere in the middle or at the very top. By putting purpose front and center, organizations achieve a profound impact on those they interact with. They energize employees, improve society, and inspire customers. Data from Boston Consulting Group (BCG)[9] indicates that, since 2005, purpose-driven organizations have grown 10 percent faster than the market. On average, brands with a strong sense of purpose have grown twice as much compared to the median growth rate. BCG expects that, until the year 2035, organizations using more purposeful language will earn total shareholder revenues that are 9 percent higher, and generate growth that is 10 percent higher, than in 2020.

The Best Time to Start Creating a New Strategy Was Yesterday. The Next Best Time Is Now!

Instead of just defining their purpose, organizations need to put purpose at the core of their strategy to reap the benefits. IMD Strategy Professor Thomas Malnight states:

"A compelling purpose clarifies what a company stands for, provides an impetus for action, and is aspirational. [. . .] Even if organizations do manage to define their purpose well, they often don't properly translate it into action - or do anything at all to fulfill it. [. . .] Leaders need to think hard about how to make purpose central to their strategy. The two best tactics for doing that are to transform the leadership agenda and to disseminate purpose throughout the organization. [. . .] By putting purpose at the core of strategy, firms can realize three specific benefits: more-unified organizations, more-motivated stakeholders, and a broader positive impact on society. [. . .] The approach to purpose [. . .] cannot be a one-off effort. Leaders need to constantly assess how purpose can guide strategy, and they need to be willing to adjust or redefine this relationship as conditions change. That demands a new kind of sustained focus, but the advantages it can confer are legion."[10]

In 2020, during the COVID-19 pandemic, global consulting firm McKinsey & Company stated: "Executives are uniquely poised at this pivotal time to bring corporate power, guided by social purpose, to the aid of millions of dislodged and vulnerable lives. Done well, their actions in this crisis can bridge, in unprecedented ways, the divide between shareholders and stakeholders in the communities they serve—and leave a lasting, positive legacy on their [. . .] identity."[11]

Before you start this journey, make certain that your purpose, desired impact, and strategy are interlaced, and make sure you are in the right state of mind. According to Bruce Simpson, CEO of the Stephen A. Schwarzman Foundation, "85% of companies have a purpose statement that doesn't mean anything to anybody. It's a fluffy statement often done by an ad agency which doesn't anchor into specific business initiatives."[12] Developing a purpose is a business exercise that requires specificity. Avoid the fluff and tie your purpose into your business strategy.

When it comes to a forward state of mind, try to be curious, apply a learner's mindset, and be non-judgmental. With an open mind, you are ready to explore the essential questions listed below, about strategy, impact, and purpose. Whatever the outcome of exploring might be, there is a chance in it for you and your leadership team to lift your strategy and thus your business to the next level. Before you continue reading the next chapters, take the self-assessment and check how well your leadership team is aligned on the existing business strategy today, and test your strategy for purpose and impact.

Strategy, Purpose, Impact: A Quick Self-Assessment

Step 1: Check for strategic alignment

- To what degree do we have a clear purpose-driven vision and business strategy in place, an agreed-on plan we are committed to, and fully invested in?

(continued)

- Are we able to link our daily work to this strategy—and do we have an aligned picture of what our strategic priorities are?
- What metrics are we checking regularly to see whether we are making good progress towards our vision?

Step 2: Test your strategy for purpose
- Is purpose the magic ingredient in the strategy? Which element(s) in our strategy make(s) our hearts glow? Hint: no glow, no purpose.
- How confidently can I articulate the magic ingredient: what goes beyond a business rationale, customer satisfaction, innovation, agility, digitalization, or other important but all too common terms?
- Which element(s) in our strategy legitimize(s) our organization in the eyes of others (e.g., our workforce and communities around us)? Note: this should go beyond making money for shareholders and employees.

Step 3: Test your strategy for impact
- Are we stopping at purpose and intent, or are we creating meaningful action?
- What is the impact we want to create by implementing our purpose-infused strategy?
- Which tangibility test can we engineer to scrutinize our strategy for impact?

Whilst exploring these questions, you'll probably find answers you are proud of and some you don't like too much. Likely, some answers will seriously challenge you. If the latter is the case, buckle up, get your team together, and create the space you need to develop your strategy and take your business to the next level.

About Alex Brueckmann

Alex is a strategy practitioner and keynote speaker who helps businesses create clarity and strategic direction. Having worked with entrepreneurs, business owners, and corporate leaders for two decades, he is a trusted advisor to businesses large and small.

Alex is the author of *The Strategy Legacy* (2023); the book introduces the business strategy and leadership framework of the Nine Elements of Organizational Identity. Corresponding resources are available on his website, such as free toolkits and online courses.

Website: www.brueckmann.ca

LinkedIn: www.linkedin.com/in/alexanderbrueckmann

The Smartest Way to Boost Profits Is Clever Pricing

Hermann Simon

Pricing, as a discipline, is relatively well understood by large companies. Intentional pricing is the most effective profit driver, making it equally important for companies of all sizes, ranging from individual entrepreneurs to large corporations. However, small and medium-sized businesses often seem to underestimate the power of pricing.

Of course, large firms are more sophisticated in pricing, although some could benefit from a more focused approach. I have been asked thousands of times what I think is the most important aspect of pricing, and my answer is always the same: *value*. Even the Romans understood this concept; they used the same term for *value* as for *price*, proving they are part and parcel. To date, the fundamental equation for pricing is *price equals value*, in the sense that the value will determine the price.

Value can be assessed based on many factors of an exchange, and thus has several definitions; it's something I take home as an entrepreneur (including the profit), and it's how a customer perceives an interaction with a seller (what they receive in exchange for payment). Finally, the value is created for suppliers. For example, when suppliers receive payment or are part of a value chain that aligns with their values. To avoid potential misunderstandings, when I use the term value in the context of pricing, there is only one relevant definition—the value the customer perceives. If price points are too far away from the perceived value, for example, if the price is too high above the value, a good or service will not sell. Whereas if the price is significantly below the appropriate value it may sell extremely well.

What we will explore in this chapter are the keys to profitable pricing:

- Focus on and quantify value-to-customer
- Only price differentiation exploits the full profit potential

- Move from one-dimensional to multidimensional prices
- Use new digital pricing schemes: dynamic, freemium, pay-per-use
- Pricing automation: use big data and artificial intelligence
- Implement a pricing process: strategy, analysis, implementation, monitoring

To Set the Right Price: First Understand the Value Drivers of Your Business

Perceived value-to-customer is driven by many determining factors: the objective product quality, brand, packaging, and interaction with the customer. Especially in the services realm, customer interaction becomes the main value driver. To meet the right price point, you should first understand the value drivers in your industry and relate them to your offering. Combined, they form the perceived value. If the value is higher than your competitor, you can charge more; if the value is lower than your competitor, you must charge less, or you will not make a profit—your offering will likely not sell. Here, you must be honest with yourself, as there is no way around it.

One way to identify the value drivers in your business is, for example, through customer surveys. However, a direct survey of value drivers and their importance for willingness to pay does not necessarily lead to the best results, as people might not tell you what they think in all honesty. Instead, the most practiced method is 'conjoint measurement', which can be easiest to understand using the example of purchasing a passenger vehicle. First, the buyer considers a series of characteristics, such as gas mileage, trim features, and price point, and then compares those characteristics to that of a car of another brand. The consumer is then confronted with potentially dozens of these paired comparisons. Based on the amassed data from these conjoint measurement surveys, we calculate how the valuation of each characteristic is weighted, from brand, design, and lifespan, to price. The key is to determine value drivers relative to price. As a result, we can predict and calculate market shares and profit models, for example, before launching new car models.

Of course, such an elaborate procedure doesn't make sense for every company. A more straightforward method is to explore value drivers by interviewing your employees, such as sales staff or service technicians, as they can assess customers and productivity. Even if this method doesn't explain everything about value drivers relative to price, it is important to understand the value drivers nonetheless. They provide insight into what is most important to a customer when making a purchasing decision. This is particularly useful when comparing your business to the competition, to compare strengths, weaknesses, and areas for improvement.

Let's say you run a small business, like a butcher shop or a hair salon. To accurately interpret the value versus the price of your goods or services, survey your customers. Devise a list of the value drivers you think are relevant to purchasing decisions for your business. Now, ask 50 to 100 customers to rank those drivers according to their importance. In addition, you should ask how they perceive your performance regarding these drivers relative to your competitors. The survey results will help you interpret your customers' priorities and make smarter pricing decisions than previously.

Differentiate Prices to Avoid Leaving Money on the Street

When we talk about the pricing of services and products, there is a maximum price point where the average buyer or user would still complete a transaction. In other words, they would likely

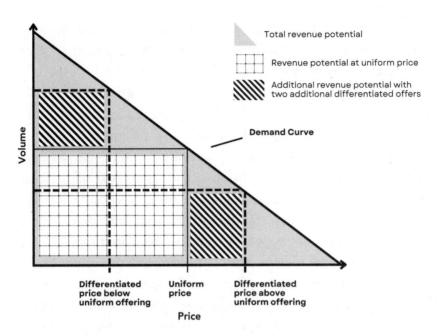

FIGURE 2.1 Additional Revenue Potential at Differentiated Price Points

still pay more than what's on the price tag. That said, businesses still sell products and services below market value because they often don't know any better, and they end up setting a price that is too low.

Differentiating prices is the most interesting challenge of pricing. If you sell at a so-called uniform price, you have only one price for a given product or service. Geometrically, the profit potential is always a triangle formed by the volume axis, the price axis, and the demand curve. If you offer at only one uniform price, you cut a rectangle out of the triangle, which is, of course, a much smaller portion than the whole triangle. The challenge is to differentiate prices to avoid leaving money on the street.

If somebody is willing to pay $120 instead of $100 (let's assume that's your price), you should have a variant of the same product that you can sell at $120 to benefit from a higher willingness to pay. You can achieve this in many ways, for example, by providing more advanced features that make a product more energy efficient, like in the case of electric cars. On the other hand, you should also have a cheaper variant of the product. This variant will attract buyers at the other end of the spectrum, who are only willing to pay $80 and wouldn't buy at your price point of $100.

Differentiating prices is the true art of pricing. It requires more information and market-specific research, however. It's not enough to know the average amount customers are willing to pay. Instead, you need to understand better the willingness to pay of an individual consumer, or at least for segments of the market.

Behind Every Price Differentiation Should Be a Product and Service Differentiation

Pricing intelligence has little to do with the size of a business. The most successful people in the pricing game are merchants in a traditional bazaar. They start a conversation with seemingly unrelated questions, like 'Which car do you drive?' If you answer 'a Ferrari,' then the merchant thinks 'Oh, this guy has money and is probably willing to pay a higher price than the average buyer'. Another question might be, 'Where do you live?' They ask questions to estimate your willingness to pay and then charge a premium price.

Even if you don't conduct elaborate customer surveys, as previously mentioned, understanding the value perception of your customers is highly important. One very effective way is to offer add-ons, such as free delivery or prolonged guarantees or services, which are not included in the base price. Differentiate your offering and offer a higher value. You will quickly establish whether a customer is willing to pay more for the higher value.

The additional value can also sit in different product components or—as often seen in industrial markets—in perceived differences in product quality, even when the product is practically the same.

Start with Value Pricing and Manage Your Business Based on Long-Term Profit

How do you arrive at your price point in the first place? Regrettably, 'cost plus' pricing is still the prevalent method. I estimate that 80 percent of the prices in the world are decided based on production cost plus a certain margin. This is what I call Marxist pricing. The most famous theory of Karl Marx is the labor value theory, where value is created through labor. He states that all costs are ultimately labor costs, even the cost of raw materials. This is why 'cost plus' pricing is reminiscent of Marxist pricing, because the cost doesn't necessarily reflect the customer's perceived value.

Let's say you build a steam engine. You can put in a lot of labor, but steam engines have become obsolete. Labor as such does not create value. It only creates value if the customer appreciates it. The certainty of cost is illusionary because it has no substantial meaning for the perceived value.

By getting rid of cost-plus pricing, you can begin identifying the value of your offering, even if it's initially uncertain and difficult. Start testing price differentiation based on certain components and add-ons to analyze what customers appreciate and are willing to pay. In that way, through trial and error, you will become better at understanding and quantifying the perceived value; ultimately, you will reach the right price.

In any case, the right price might not necessarily be the highest price possible. Even if value equals price, as mentioned previously, it doesn't mean that alternatively charging *less* than the perceived value can't be done. Let's assume your product is 20 percent better than a competitor's comparable product. Instead of charging a 20 percent price premium, I advise charging only 10 percent more. You should not fully exploit the value potential but share it with your customers, to create additional value, repeat business, or brand loyalty.

No Company That Turned a Profit Ever Went Bankrupt

This insight should have substantial implications on how you manage your business. It's best to manage your company in a profit-oriented way, based on long-term profit. Profit orientation is the only meaningful goal because it observes both the market and the cost side simultaneously. It's important to keep in mind that amongst the three profit drivers—sales volume, price, and cost—price is the most effective. If you increase the price of a typical industrial product or service by 1 percent your profit will increase by 10 percent. The profit multiplier of price is 10.

For sales volume, the multiplier is only 4, and for cost, it is 6. So, why is it so much lower for the volume increase? Because with increasing volume, your costs increase; that's what we call marginal costs and they typically eat up 60 percent of the increase in revenue. So, if you have 10 percent more, minus 60 percent of 10 percent, you are at 40 percent, or a multiplier of 4.

Increasing your prices by 1 percent is usually doable. For example, a global market leader in assembly products gave incentives to their sales team to get more firm on discounts. Within three months, they observed an average discount decrease from 16 percent to 14 percent, without any loss in volume or loss in customers. That's two percentage points more profit margin or an increase in price of 2 percent. This change resulted in an increase of several $100 million per year, a seemingly tiny piece in the equation that turned into a huge profit impact.

Remember that the most effective way to increase profit is to eliminate profit killers, such as price wars. Other profit killers include setting the wrong goals: revenue, volume, market share, market dominance, and beating the competition. Additionally, company-internal goal conflicts, wrong incentives, or neglecting costs are also capable of destroying profits.

Business Owners Should Measure Profit as Economic Profit

How do you successfully measure profit in your business today? What are the key performance indicators? Earnings before interest and taxes (EBIT), or maybe EBITDA (similar to EBIT, and adding depreciation and amortization)? Both are commonly used. And there are some interesting custom-made indicators like WeWork and the "Community Adjusted EBITDA," which includes marketing expenditures. We can also look at Uber and their "Core Platform Contribution Profit" and Groupon's "Adjusted Consolidated Segment Operating Income." Each of these business examples has one thing in common: deception and fogging. They share little in regard to their true profit. To successfully measure your company's profit, you should use a higher benchmark: economic profit. It is the profit that exceeds the cost of capital, otherwise known as the Weighted Average Cost of Capital (WACC).

Economic profit goes hand-in-hand with *entrepreneurial* profit. Without an economic profit, an entrepreneur would be wiser to invest their capital in the market than to run a business. Don't be deceived; true profit is only what your business can keep after it has met all contractually agreed upon claims of employees, suppliers, banks, and the state. If you are serious about profit, you should use economic profit as your benchmark.

Price Increases Are Easier in Times of Inflation, But Watch Out for Phantom Profits

Inflation is back in a big way. In 2022, the annual inflation rate reached 8 percent in the US. We must expect inflation to stay, and we may even reach similar levels as seen during the 1970s, which were characterized by *stagflation* (stagnation and inflation combined). At that time, the oil crises in 1973 and 1978 were the triggers for raising prices. Today, several factors have led to inflation: COVID-19 and the accompanying explosion in money supply, the disruptions in global supply chains, and the Ukraine crisis. All these factors are causing the prices of energy, raw materials, and food to rise exponentially.

The inflation traffic light is deep red. In this situation, it's easy to make catastrophic pricing mistakes. However, there are also methods to escape relatively unscathed if you get the pricing right. The greatest risk posed by inflationary developments is implementing the necessary price increases too late or not at all. It is near impossible to catch up after missing these opportunities.

Inflation involves a problem that is rarely considered and not well understood, *phantom profits*. When prices and costs rise proportionally, nominal profits also rise. But this higher nominal profit is not worth more than the profit before inflation. If you adjust nominal profit for inflation, you arrive at the so-called *real profit*. In periods of relatively low inflation, such as between 1990 and 2020, the difference between nominal and real profit is marginal. However, that was not the case in the 1970s. The annual inflation rate was above 6 percent between 1971 and 1982. And today, at the beginning of the 2020s, we are seeing inflation rates of the same magnitude.

Taxes are levied against nominal profit. The phantom profits are, therefore, subject to taxation, even though they do not contribute to an increase in real value. In times of high inflation, companies should strive to protect their real profit and not get blinded by the allure of phantom profits. This means that you must use current procurement costs and not historical costs for your pricing.

Ten Commandments for Pricing in Times of Inflation

1. React quickly because inflation is here to stay.
2. Pay attention to the inflation rate in your market, not to the general rate.
3. Price increases are made easier by inflation.
4. Inflation reveals how strong your pricing power is. If it is weak, you need to improve your pricing power through innovation, branding, and so on.
5. You must understand your customers; on the one hand, they are trying to find bargains; on the other hand, they are perturbed by the wave of price increases.
6. Don't wait until all competitors have increased prices; rather, act earlier.

7. Do not raise your prices below the inflation rate, but rather slightly above it.

8. Whether you can fully pass on cost increases depends on the behavior of your competitors. Full pass-through is often difficult.

9. Jumping over price barriers (such as $10 or $10,000) is easier in inflation.

10. Stay on the ball. If inflation continues, adjust your prices at short intervals.

Strong Changes in Currency Exchange Rates Can Add or Offset Inflation Risks

Dealing with inflation is already challenging enough for companies. In addition, there is the risk of strongly fluctuating currency exchange rates. Let's take the almost 8 percent inflation in the USA mentioned earlier. In addition, the US dollar gained approximately 10 percent in value against the Euro between March 2021 and March 2022. For a European company buying goods or raw materials in the US, that equates to a combined price increase of 18 percent. There is no way around passing through at least some of these cost increases to your own prices. But will the willingness of customers change due to inflation and the rise in the value of the dollar?

It will. When customers see that your prices have increased, as in this example, because goods are coming from the US, they will also consider that they have inflation in the Eurozone. You can therefore assume that there is a shift in willingness to pay. Ultimately, inflation and currency losses are cost increases that you should impart to customers. However, it's not always fool-proof, as a part of these cost increases will likely have to be absorbed by your business. A worsening procurement situation usually affects profits, at least partly.

In this market environment, American businesses have a twofold advantage. If they source exclusively in the US, they only deal with inflation-based cost increases and the challenge of passing them through. Additionally, businesses can take advantage of the devalued Euro, for example, to buy services in the Eurozone at a lower price than before. Combining these two agents can protect their profits.

Time is a critical factor here. If disruptions are more of a temporary nature, companies are reluctant because the costs of the changeover are too high in relation to the short-term benefit they gain. However, if the shifts are permanent, for example, due to better productivity than in your own country, then it follows to buy externally. Businesses should think these changes through, and consider inflation, exchange rates, and trade barriers as actual costs.

Whether the prices change for customers also depends on the strategy and the pricing power of a company. A company can certainly say that it would like its products to have relatively stable market prices and thus refrain from passing on large-scale cost increases. Another company might avoid currency risks by always issuing invoices in its home currency. However, this is not always optimal because it shifts the risk to the customer. Ultimately, it is about the distribution of cost risks between the supplier and the buyer. If the customer isn't willing to take that risk, they won't buy anymore. One way of mitigating the currency risk for both sides is to procure goods and services in the customer's currency.

The Future of Pricing Is Driven by Big Data and AI

Let's look into the future of pricing. We have several impacts of modern technology on pricing. One is big data. In the past, we had very little data. When I wrote my doctoral dissertation forty years ago, researchers were starving for data. Today, we are drowning in data and the challenge is to extract the pertinent information from a bottomless pool. Artificial intelligence can help us synthesize information. As part of a project in the fast-food sector, we fed tons of data into a system and an artificial intelligence discovered some very strange and unexpected correlations. For instance, certain sports had a very strong effect on promotions in cities where these sports events took place. We would never have detected this correlation without using AI.

But even without these sophisticated methods, smaller companies, especially, should embrace the power of pricing. If you are selling online, for example using a web shop, it's very easy to test different prices. It's relatively inexpensive to introduce a dynamic pricing system.

For instance, when you notice that willingness to pay fluctuates throughout the day, because different people buy in the evening than in the morning, you can consider adjusting your prices, on different scales of a day or a season. You can also measure the effect of promotions quite easily and effectively.

Let's assume you sell mobile phones, and today, you charge $500 for a phone, tomorrow $400, and in two days $600. Immediately, within days, you see how many phones you sell at a given price point. You created a demand curve that allows you to choose the best price among these three prices. Experimenting is a very important indicator.

Competitive prices are another key factor. What do competitors charge for the same phone? Differentiation is not only a question of the product but also of communication and having the right distribution. But there are more sophisticated methods as well. Let's use the example of the 'BahnCard', which Simon-Kucher & Partner created for Deutsche Bahn, the German railway corporation. The card costs about €500 annually. Benefits include a 50 percent discount on all tickets purchased for the duration of a year. All of a sudden, traveling by car wasn't cheaper than using the train anymore. Car travel was the competitor, so Deutsche Bahn had to look for ways to compete with the car. Deutsche Bahn sells more than 6 million units every year. The card creates customer loyalty because customers see it as an opportunity to make back their upfront payment.

Choose the Right Pricing System to Determine the Optimal Price and Capture Value

Staying with Deutsche Bahn, the BahnCard is a two-dimensional pricing system. You pay for the card, and the tickets. Amazon Prime is also an example of a two-dimensional pricing system, in which payment is made by a monthly fee that qualifies you for different product prices and services compared to non-paying customers. We are seeing more and more of these multidimensional pricing systems emerge. My advice is not just to look at the price as such, but to find different systems that help you to differentiate your pricing.

Is the price too high or too low? This frequently asked question is pedestrian and could be improved by asking if your pricing system is optimal. How do we differentiate prices? Should products and prices be bundled? Is dynamic pricing, where prices are continuously adjusted, effective? Instead of a one-dimensional price, should we have a multidimensional price scheme? Instead of a sales model, could we implement a subscription model? Do customers prefer pay-per-use over flat rates? Is it possible to charge performance-based prices? There are an infinite number of variations, but a lot more observation and data is required to optimize them.

Eventually, you will naturally aim to gather the information that quantifies value-to-customer. It is the core of pricing and the only way to fully optimize price. Great progress has already been made with methods such as conjoint measurement. Measurement methods will continue to improve, leading to more valid and differentiated quantifications of value-to-customer.

The Boundaries of Pricing Are Ethical and Political, Less Economical

Considering the future of pricing, we should also examine the ethical perspective of pricing. In general, when customers and suppliers are playing on a level playing field, prices are ethical. We see shifts toward unethical behavior when suppliers have a monopolistic position. For instance, in the case of an emergency, when they abuse their position and sell necessary goods at extremely elevated prices. This is unethical.

Of course, there are extremely difficult cases, such as the pricing of life-saving drugs. There are drugs that heal life-threatening diseases, which have not been curable to date with one injection. The cost of these drugs can be extremely high—the most expensive costing around $2 million. Of course, this leads to a difficult question that cannot be answered: what is the value of human life? While this is an extreme case, under normal conditions, in fair competition, prices are ethical.

It seems that prices are moving into areas that traditionally went without prices. These increasingly include education, the environment, parts of the health sector, and other public services. These expansions of price contain the potential for social tension.

In exchange for a higher price, does one get faster lanes on roads or reserved parking spaces? Do people receive preferential treatment for higher prices, such as at airport security checkpoints? Can only the wealthy afford environmentally harmful behavior? Economically, such pricing systems make a lot of sense, both financially and in terms of control. Politically, they are explosive.

About Hermann Simon

Hermann is the Founder, former co-CEO, and Honorary Chairman of the global consulting firm Simon-Kucher & Partners. He is one of the most important management thinkers in the world. Simon taught at universities in Germany and was a visiting professor at Harvard Business School, Stanford, London Business School, INSEAD, Keio University Tokyo, and Massachusetts Institute of Technology. He has published more than 35 books in 27 languages, including the global bestsellers *Hidden Champions* and *Power Pricing*. His latest books are *True Profit! No Company Ever Went Broke from Turning a Profit* (2021) and *Beating Inflation* (2022).

Website: www.hermannsimon.com

LinkedIn: www.linkedin.com/in/simonhermann

3

Creating Value and a Sustainable Impact for Your Business

Sheetal Khullar

When I started collaborating with business leaders on sustainability, I was surprised to find them playing defense. It wasn't long before I realized that the inherent challenges of understanding and adopting value creation were holding them back from leveraging opportunities that I was able to foresee.

Business leaders are often faced with skepticism when addressing sustainability and profits. The conversation generally leans towards costs. In my practice, I have enjoyed witnessing some brilliant transformations that occur when leadership switches focus to sustainability as a lever to change and a pathway toward the future.

My goal is to share insights on:

- How sustainable business practices can help create value.

- How, as business leaders, you can transform your current operations to benefit the planet.

- How to leverage your good work to build a powerful and transformative business and brand.

We have all experienced the power of a successful business idea and its ability to invigorate curiosity and passion. It energizes us to rally support and keeps us motivated to nourish and sustain goals. When the same idea connects itself to purpose, it lays the foundations for a sustainable business. Needless to say that the words—curiosity, passion, and purpose—also form the foundational pillars of any sustainability-related change in business.

Purpose inherently lies at the core of your business; identifying it requires a deep dive into your mission and values. Simply defined, purpose is the need you fulfill for those you serve. *Need*, in this case, isn't limited to the physical product and its use but also includes the psychological, societal, environmental, and economic fulfillment it generates. When measured, it is called *value*.

This chapter will guide you through defining, creating, aligning, and communicating value.

Defining Value

Value creation is a dedicated and combined effort across the value chain and is led best by an openness to change and a problem-solving approach.

The concept of creating value is not unknown to businesses. After all, firms have generated wealth for decades, building systems to ensure its distribution through the value chain—including suppliers, manufacturers, employees, investors, business partners, and consumers, with the argument being that since these groups are the enablers, they should also be the beneficiaries.

In the meantime, businesses forgot to consider one of their most significant stakeholders, the planet, whose generosity and resources they have abundantly utilized. This is where the concept of creating value comes in. It involves including the planet and society on your list of enablers, understanding their contributions, and ensuring that they benefit every step of the way.

Your question to me at this juncture might be—*how do I do that?*

After all, you have a business to run, employees to pay, products to launch, and investors to keep happy. Would a dive into value creation mode steer you away from your goal?

My answer to you would be—*it's best not to think linear.*

Let us consider an example of a product launch. The teams have put in the effort in creating the concept from material to launch. Your value chain is defined and go-to-market resources have been accounted for. You now have two ways of looking at your value chain: upstream and downstream. Where would you like to activate the value creation mode?

Of course, if you are a sustainable business, you would have taken care of, or at least started to investigate your upstream emissions, waste, and water usage. In that case, you are already creating value by managing the planetary resources you use each day. However, many businesses find evaluating their downstream operations an easy first step toward sustainability.

Looking at your product's positioning is often a great place to start. Forming consumer associations that go beyond the direct use of the product creates a significant impact. Impactful products add to a wholesome brand image and ensure high customer return and credibility.

Heineken, a well-known beer company, understands its power as it helps bring people together. The brand aligned its marketing campaign to remind people to socialize responsibly during the pandemic. Their ad campaign[13] serves as an excellent example of how products can address social behaviors in a light-hearted way while continuing to promote and sell.

Amongst the brands addressing the issue of single-use plastic is Single Use Ain't Sexy, founded by Josh Howard.[14] It has taken up much of Australia's social media and billboard space with messaging that is direct, eye-catching, and fun. Recipient of the Good Design Award in 2021, the brand is helping consumers make a mindset shift from purchasing single-use plastic to using a refillable option instead. This is yet another example of how business goals, when linked to purpose, can have a transformative impact on value creation.

The contributions of both these brands highlight the importance of understanding the social need your product could address or the environmental issue it could support. Consumers respond positively and wholeheartedly to products that credibly show their contribution to solving some of the world's pressing issues.

As a business, it's essential to note your consumer's preferences regarding competitive price and quality. To profit, you must meet their demands, which begs the question: how can we create models that integrate value without increasing margins or compromising on quality?

Before addressing this question, we should define what we mean by a sustainable business.

A sustainable business shapes its business models to benefit stakeholders, the environment, and society. It does not steer away from challenges; instead, it embraces them by focusing efforts on enabling and creating pathways for growth and innovation.

Creating Value

Creating value requires thinking beyond what lies in our straight line of vision. The concepts that follow will help you explore this further. I would recommend keeping a product in mind as you read. It could belong to your business or another but must be something you have used or helped create.

Thinking Circular

Circularity involves moving away from the *take-make-waste* model of consumption toward reducing waste substantially by turning it back into a product. A great example here is Carib Glassworks, a Caribbean glass company that encourages consumers to recycle used glass bottles and containers by placing them in community bins.[15] These are then collected and reused to produce fresh glass. Making recycling and renewing options available for consumers ensures the product ends up in the right hands while taking the initiative to educate the consumer helps create systemic shifts in the marketplace.

With Scope 3 carbon emissions[16] becoming a rising concern, businesses need to be mindful of the products they design and where they end up after use—also known as a product's life cycle.

Firms that endorse the concept of circular thinking gain enormously as they innovate and lead the way. These companies seek efficient methods of using resources while saving on costs. It is much easier to *think circular* when the product is on the design table. The biggest challenge lies in creating a closed loop for a product already on the market. With billions of products out there, the focus should now shift to ensuring that they don't pile up as waste going forward.

It is essential for product teams to analyze their designs and understand what aspects can be made sustainable—be it recyclable, biodegradable, or simply renewable and plugged into use for someone else.

A UK-based start-up, Bio Bean, has found innovative ways of using coffee waste.[17] They offer coffee recycling solutions to address the challenge of disposing of coffee grounds sustainably, thereby creating biodegradable products and contributing to the circular economy. The idea is that someone's waste has the potential to be another's resource.

Adopting circularity requires it to be viewed as a cost-saving instead of a capital expense. A sustained focus on improvising processes that reduce and capture waste form the basis for adopting closed-loop practices. This leads us to the critical point of cost savings and efficiencies.

It is a constant endeavor for companies to become efficient, with many turning to technology in place of human capital. At what stage of business planning should you consider the impact of your business operations, and how could you make decisions that support positive contributions? Venture builders will tell you that it is ideal to do so at the design stage, and I agree.

Reinventing and reengineering operations can be a tedious and slow process.

> Efficiencies can create a perfect and fertile ground for a regenerative business conscious of the planetary boundaries and of preserving what it consumes.

Thinking Efficiencies

As a first step, assess your current operations and highlight areas that consume more than they should. Eventually, you'll be able to pinpoint high costs and wastes to avoid.

Consumption is a key criterion—it can be easily tracked, benchmarked, and analyzed to understand waste patterns. Additionally, the more we view business as a consumer of resources, the more mindful we will be when we overproduce or over-create, ultimately making us more accountable.

One of the 17 UN Sustainable Development Goals that speaks the loudest to me is SDG 12: Responsible Production and Consumption.[18] It states that if we continue consuming the way we currently do, and should the global population reach 9.6 billion, the equivalent of almost three planets could be required to sustain our current lifestyles.

Businesses keen on finding sustainable production solutions must consume less while encouraging similar consumer behavior. They could do so by observing the patterns of production and waste, using climate-friendly materials and processes to lessen their negative impact, and developing newer business models that help keep products in the value chain for longer.

As a business leader, consider if your business operations are well aligned with responsible consumption. Are your production and waste cycles monitored to benefit the planet? If not, how could they be improved?

Exploring the work of companies such as Allbirds and Patagonia establishes the importance of considering the climate and social footprint of businesses every step of the way. It is easy for a business to impact the planet negatively should it not be intentional or mindful in its approach.

A value chain assessment exercise will help identify and quantify the red flags (high emission and consumption zones) and the gaps (high waste and cost-intensive zones) in your business operations. Once you have conducted the exercise and gained clarity, begin with a simple step of sorting.

"Should Do," "Could Do," and "Don't Know How to Do"

Start by putting the highlighted zones in one of these three categories:

Should Do's: These include processes that have the maximum impact on your climate footprint, such as procurement, energy, and water use.

Addressing these is crucial as they make your business carbon-intensive. Then there are easy-to-do transformations such as moving to biodegradable and low plastic packaging, which guarantee quick turnarounds and pain-free implementations. Another area where businesses find the shift easier is plugging into renewable energy for their operations.

The challenging aspect of most value chains is the suppliers. It is one thing to be able to transform your operations, but another to have someone transform theirs. I recommend a transparent learning- and profit-based approach with suppliers because the more they understand your sustainability goals and plans, the more likely they are to help you find efficient solutions. Products with a carbon-intensive upstream often grapple with issues involving pace and performance within their supplier base.

A recent conversation between Helena Helmersson, CEO of H&M, and Jesper Brodin, CEO of IKEA, has highlighted the challenge of companies with suppliers in emerging markets still using fossil fuels. This reaffirms the fact that we must engage with suppliers with clarity and purposeful missions.[19]

Could Do's: These are less carbon-intensive processes that could be put on the back burner until you address the more pressing issues. It is hard to determine these on a general level as they would be specific to each business. An example would be the carbon footprint associated with travel. If you are a local business, you would likely have a relatively low travel carbon footprint; therefore, it can be put lower on your list of priorities.

Don't Know How to Do's: Surprisingly, this list can be quite long. These aspects of your business significantly impact climate, but you don't necessarily have the in-house capability to address them.

An example of this is when you cannot find a suitable 'end-of-use' of your product, or you want solutions to your material sourcing in ways that regenerate the environment. On occasions such as these, you can always turn to collaborations.

Thinking Partnerships

Successful partnerships have an unbound potential to create, solve, and take risks. Partnerships are most effective when they work towards a shared vision. Partners must complement rather than compete while committing to trying new solutions within a specified timeline. Collaborations can bring up complexities of thought and insecurities, leading to a mindset of distrust and no-go situations. A better way would be to choose partners who appreciate your business strengths and are happy to help you build while mutually benefitting.

Partnerships provide solutions to problems that businesses alone cannot solve. Many of these challenges lie within the ecosystem, therefore, becoming the responsibility of all. Governments, too, are leaning towards the multi-stakeholder model for problem-solving and value creation as these are effective, help share responsibilities, and in most cases when executed well, are profitable for all.

We can see an example of shared responsibility in the development of hydrogen as an energy resource. Investments from both the public and private sectors are being matched with technology and infrastructure from energy companies to produce hydrogen.

Consider what aspect of sustainability you are currently being challenged by and how collaborations might assist you.

The race to net-zero has given birth to a unique set of start-ups and ventures focused on creating solutions to problems businesses face during transition. These solutions range from calculating carbon emissions to restructuring supply chains and advising on carbon offsets. Consider how you could work together with them.

I want you to revisit the concept of creating value: think of a partner you could collaborate with and determine the value you would collectively bring to each other, and the industry at large. To propel your thought process, here is an example of a brand partnership that has established itself quite firmly and successfully—Adidas and Parley for the Oceans. These partners have turned plastic ocean waste into material fit enough to create a sustainable fashion line, thereby revolutionizing the industry.

As a business leader, it's essential to think about what you want to gain the most out of your collaborations. Not all partnerships are about diversifying products or adding newer markets. As in this example, they can also be about finding solutions. Bringing your best team forward and engaging with your partner with openness and clarity can solve several sustainability riddles.

Collaborations also help leverage the strength of each partner to create an impact within the ecosystem and, if successful, can invite more players to contribute and gain. A great example of circularity is Nespresso's recent partnership with Zéta, which has led to zero-waste sneakers being made from coffee grounds.

Having reaffirmed that circular thinking, efficient operations, and partnerships are excellent value creation modes, we must act to combine them in a way that benefits the bottom line and gains the support of all stakeholders. Stakeholders need a clear understanding of your sustainability goals and challenges. They need to be aligned with your thinking and understand the pressing needs of the business and its impact. In other words, they must know what you know. Transparency in sustainability is quickly taking precedence, more in some industries than others; for example, the fashion industry continues to remain under pressure to disclose its supply chains both for social and environmental impact.

Taking stakeholders along and establishing trust from the very start is a far more lucrative way of working than simply publishing reports and expecting them to follow and agree. Brands and businesses that have held themselves accountable for such transparency have had stakeholders far more forgiving of their failures and more accepting of green products.

Let us take a moment to reflect on your stakeholders and the relationships you share with them. How could you gain a deeper understanding of the problems they face? Some of the social and environmental concerns that affect world communities at large include gender inequality, lack of safe drinking water, and quality of education. It is essential for a business that operates in multiple markets to know and address the needs of its communities and consumers.

Aligning Value

The following section will help further your knowledge on how you might seek alignment between the value you create and your stakeholders' priorities. In my conversations with business leaders, we often stumble upon the concept of aligning sustainability goals with the UN SDGs, while also evaluating how collaborations might assist.

Collaborations help facilitate the goals, but your firm's alignment with the SDGs must be an internal exercise that keeps all stakeholders in mind. Materiality assessments are a great way of understanding what aspects of ESG—environmental, social, and corporate governance—concern your stakeholders the most.[20] Nestle conducts these assessments regularly, as they believe it helps the business prioritize issues. The assessments are published on their website for all stakeholders to see and follow, a great initiative toward being transparent and inclusive.

Assessments keep key stakeholders in perspective, categorizing them as either internal or external. Their opinions and choices on what a business should prioritize are included in data-driven analysis, then structured to produce a materiality matrix that highlights the issues in order of perceived urgency. Companies have witnessed issues ranging from diversity, equity, and inclusion to climate goals and health highlighted as some of the most urgent issues.

Most businesses engage with SDGs from the viewpoint of the planetary resources they impact the most. However, that doesn't necessarily bring everyone on board. We will explore this further in the next section.

Interface, a modular flooring company, is committed to experimenting with renewable and recyclable materials for sustainable production. They have had unprecedented success in reducing their carbon footprint and have adopted the mission of 'LIVE ZERO' every day. They are constantly looking for creative problem solvers to join their team.

Sustainability and its challenges need the problem-solvers and design thinkers to step up and help. Look for good problem solvers in your business, regardless of their role. Reach out to them and have them look into what might be currently challenging your sustainability goals.

Mauro Porcini, SVP and Chief Design Officer at Pepsico, and Joe Gebbia, Co-founder of Airbnb, have been featured in a podcast on product design and innovation. This episode showcases the passion and creative skills of the two leaders. They highlight the fact that design thinking and problem-solving cannot be kept apart, not anymore, as the solutions to circularity often lie amongst them.[21]

As you prepare to be a transformative leader and overcome some of the steep challenges that may lie ahead, you should also consider communicating about all the good work you are doing. Like any new endeavor, establishing contact with your consumers early in the process helps build up interest, excitement, and most importantly, credibility.

Consumers are often surprised when businesses and brands publish sustainability reports without any precursor to the initiatives. What are the key parameters to be mindful of when communicating value? What should businesses be wary of and what are the common pitfalls?

Communicating Value

What does a consumer truly value regarding their environmental and social impact?

Your company's communications and PR operations play a vital role in helping them make that connection. Consumers want the product to be ethical and not harm the planet. More importantly, they want the product to align with their greatest concerns. Until now, businesses have held price, quality, and ease of purchase to be the key consumer concerns. Businesses must further endeavor to fully understand the social and environmental issues that impact consumers.

Airbnb.org, a non-profit organization supported by Airbnb, opens homes at times of crisis to those in need. It serves as an example of a business understanding what its consumers are most impacted by and then using its resources to make a difference.[22]

The next thing your consumer needs from you is clarity. They want to understand how you are helping the planet and why they should take you seriously. They want to see consistency and a deep sense of purpose. Communicating with them does not have to be a matrix of reports and testimonials, but clear storytelling works.

There is also the responsibility of showing progression. A consumer who witnesses your genuine and credible efforts would gladly be your ambassador. By communicating with the consumer, you are helping them broaden their vision while inspiring them to make the right choice.

Businesses often avoid educating their stakeholders simply because they don't know the benefits. I am here to tell you that there is immense benefit in investing time and resources into building stronger consumer associations. A great example is Oatly, a company with outstanding communication and marketing expertise. Their style is factual, conversational, easy to comprehend, and fun to read. Although I may not be an oat milk enthusiast, I have always admired their commitment to sustainability and their passion for connection.

Communication with the consumer is just as important as deciding what aspects of your sustainability journey will interest them. Broadly speaking, there are three aspects that concern a consumer—the environmental and social objective, the overarching goal, and the innovative way you achieved it. Therefore, it's important to share how you reach your goals, and the challenges you overcome along the way.

Some brands and businesses are doing this effectively; there are also several who, despite the good work done, are so focused on sharing their net-zero vision that they are missing the opportunity to share their story. Oil and gas companies are the most susceptible to this pattern. While they are overly conscious of communicating their climate vision and goals, they lose the real opportunity of engaging with the consumer.

The 3E Model for Impact

Having witnessed several brands face the challenge of creating a meaningful connection with their consumer, I developed the 3E Model for Impact (see Figure 3.1). The model provides businesses a structured approach to leverage and communicate their good work and create transformational impact and growth.

Educate

Most consumers look specifically to brands to help them fill the knowledge gap and make decisions that will benefit the planet. Assist your consumers by sharing sustainability-led information and data that quantifies your positive impact as the first step to open and transparent communication.

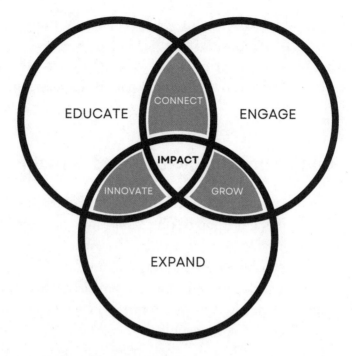

FIGURE 3.1 The 3E Model for Impact

Engage

Consumer touchpoints are an essential means of dispersing information. These touchpoints become a regular point of contact between the business and the customer. You can flood them with discount options or decide to create a more intentional space for learning, developing, and benefiting from one another. Encourage your consumer to ask questions, leave feedback, and share concerns to allow them to participate in your sustainability drive.

Expand

Build partnerships that help your brand become more effective and connected. Every partnership is a way to expand your consumers' positive contributions to society and the environment. Corona beer has done so successfully by committing to remove

1 million pounds of plastic from beaches and its business by 2025, through its partnership with Oceanic Global.

Having implemented this model successfully across industry sectors, I have found it to deliver on 3 counts: connection, innovation, and growth.

Connection, Innovation, and Growth

Learning-led consumer engagement builds authentic connections and trust. King Arthur Baking Company engages with its consumers by providing them with a platform to share recipes. Over the years, they have built a strong community of bakers who are loyal to their products and mission. Similarly, when coupled with learning, partnerships inspire innovation. They provide the incentive to ideate and solve problems together.

Growth happens when the power of engagement is coupled with expansion. Memobottle, an Australian brand, has a commitment to providing clean drinking water with every Memobottle sold. As of this writing, it has provided over 22 million days of clean water access and diverted more than 100 million single-use bottles from landfills. The brand has witnessed positive growth and its partnership with water.org towards solving the water crisis globally has certainly been appreciated by its current and potential consumers.

As a business leader, you will face the dilemma of what to share and what perhaps might be an unnecessary detail. A guiding thought that has served me well is putting myself in the consumer's shoes and coming from a place of intent and vision. Your vision, coupled with the passion and skills of your stakeholders, will create the roadmap for your business's sustainable future.

As we close this chapter, I would like you to direct some thought toward the essence of time and the fact that there is still much to do. I always encourage leaders to embed sustainability and its practice into their daily decision-making.

There aren't any excuses left for not taking care of what we must preserve; doing so with passion, pride, and purpose makes for an enjoyable ride.

About Sheetal Khullar

Sheetal is a business strategist who's passionate about sustainable development and impact. Her expertise lies in defining growth and ESG strategies for the consumer, finance, and technology sectors. She has designed sustainability management systems for start-ups and SMEs across APAC.

With more than a decade of experience in corporate business development, leading social sector organizations, and strategy consulting, she believes that businesses with a well-defined purpose can help alleviate some of the world's societal and environmental challenges.

Sheetal is a contributor to the *Financial Times*, Sustainable Views portal, and is also a Global Sustainability Advocate supporting start-ups and social enterprises dedicated to the UN SDGs.

LinkedIn: www.linkedin.com/in/sheetalkhullar

II

How Businesses Shape Impactful Cultures Through Leadership

Moving away from the three essential hard skills for entrepreneurs, business owners, and corporate leaders, there is one more skill that is essential for success: leadership. In countless leadership coaching sessions with clients, I have observed that many business owners underestimate the importance of leadership. They don't necessarily see how they lead. They often tell me something along the lines of not having much of a team to lead. They fall back on the misconception that there's not much you can do in a small part of the sandbox.

These sentiments are noted in leaders of large organizations as well as small business owners. During our coaching sessions, they eventually arrive at a broader definition of leadership, inspired by John Maxwell, who said, "The true measure of leadership is influence—nothing more, nothing less." By that definition, we are all leading in one way or another. We all make choices that influence others, just by how we show up at meetings with clients, suppliers, or employees. How we treat people and our planet has an effect. When we act as leaders, we contribute to shaping more equitable workplaces and society.

Theme II is about leadership and culture, especially through the lens of leading businesses through some of the most pressing issues of our time. We are leading through disruption, creating people centric high-performance cultures, closing the talent gap, and using conflict as a source for growth.

We live in an age of disruption, which makes people feel out of control. We want to know our place and how we fit in, while seeking guidance from leaders to help us find a way forward. Businesses can create a sense of identity and that helps us embrace the discomfort of disruption. *New York Times* bestselling author, Charlene Li, shares ten easy-to-apply rules for leading through disruption, and for cultivating the right environment for innovation.

Ultimately, there is a need to measure every business against its ability to perform and deliver results. No matter your industry, how you define and achieve performance matters. If you think about financial performance metrics, like profit, yes, these are lagging indicators for performance. They are measurable after finishing the job. And there are a few indicators that show you whether you are well positioned for success. To prepare ourselves for success in leadership is Dr. Terry Jackson, a Thinkers50 leader and member of the Marshall Goldsmith 100 Coaches. Jackson shares six components that business leaders should equip their teams with to build people-centric high-performance cultures at work.

The COVID-19 pandemic accelerated certain workforce trends such as shortages of leadership talent and labor. We feel the consequences every day, when products or services we considered as essential now are either not available at all or only at a price premium. Angela Howard, an organizational psychologist and culture strategist, explores with us the intersection of modern leadership, culture, and your desired impact in the world. Her approach will support you in building workplaces and businesses that are more diverse, equitable, and inclusive, which will ultimately help you bridge the talent and leadership gaps.

Change, disruption, and transformation shake things up and often cause conflict among colleagues. They also cause conflict between businesses and their stakeholders, like employees, boards of directors, and clients. The potential sources for conflict are endless and you are likely experiencing conflict to some extent daily, in your personal and professional lives. Fostering learning and generating growth means sometimes provoking positive conflict to find the best way forward; it is a critical capability for leaders. Jerry Fu, a conflict resolution coach and Doctor of Pharmacy, shares with us how to reframe conflict into opportunities for learning and resolution. He introduces a step-by-step process that you can adopt for handling the next conflict ahead.

4

Mastering Disruption and the Future of Work

Charlene Li

Disruption is one of those buzzwords we have heard a lot lately, *but why?* Because it's a great way to create fresh takes on old problems, and to find answers to the challenges we face. Disruption means creating more efficient solutions in our target markets. Then we can resolve those unmet needs instead of focusing on winning awards or accolades for innovation.

We can think of disruptors in the tech industry, startups in Silicon Valley, and most recently, supply chain disruptions during and after the effects of the COVID-19 pandemic as examples. Humans see disruption tear us away from our understanding of the status quo, our relationships with each other, and where we are situated in the world. As a result of no longer knowing where to stand, we feel confused, unsure, and disrupted.

Disruption typically makes people feel out of control. And until we figure out where and how we fit in the greater scheme of things, we will continue to feel disrupted. Instinctively, our feelings tell us to get rid of this discomfort as soon as possible.

Disruptors Lead the Way

Changing the status quo in business means shaking things up, innovating, and creating disruption.

Look at businesses such as Netflix. When everyone thought we'd continue making the weekly trek to Blockbuster for the next VHS and then DVD, Netflix, a true disruptor and leader in streaming services, came in guns blazing. Netflix and other streaming services effectively sunk the in-store movie rental industry, rendering it obsolete. Now, they are creating ongoing disruption in the entertainment industry at large, with the ever-growing cancellation of cable subscriptions around the world. Not only that, but they have forever changed how we produce movies and TV series.

Another great example of disruption emerged out of necessity during the COVID-19 pandemic. Businesses worldwide were forced to shut down for fear of spreading the virus. Amid the many rolling lockdowns, going to the office as we once had was impossible, so companies with offices had to think fast. Virtually all businesses adopted a work-from-home model (WFH). Entire companies learned how to navigate their daily meetings using Zoom and create new workflows with Customer Relationship Management (CRM) platforms and other software.

Leaders naturally worried that this new WFH model would mean lowered productivity and poor results from their direct reports. As a matter of fact, the opposite has been found to be true.[23] Employees working from home saw as much as a 13 percent increase in productivity. Just think, no more water-cooler chats, increased focus time, and quicker and more effective communication.

When companies began to transition back to an in-office model, we saw push-back from employees; there really was no need for everyone to go back. We saw employees leaving long-standing roles to join companies that fully and permanently adopted a WFH policy.

How Do We Make It Easier?

The disruptors are accustomed to change because they've adapted to a disruptor's mindset. They have decided that they aren't going to run away from uncomfortable feelings or situations because it allows them to help more people. It makes them more agile and enables them to implement the changes needed to thrive in an ever-changing world.

Disruption is an opportunity for growth, rather than a threat, and the sooner we can jump on board, the sooner we can use it to our advantage. With the speed of changes occurring at a much faster rate than ever before, we have to learn how to thrive while uncomfortable, rather than be debilitated. There is real value in feeling discomfort and being pulled away from the norms of your business; there's benefit in living, even temporarily, in chaos.

To Be Competitive, Innovation Is No Longer Enough

It's essential to adopt a strategy for disruptive growth. Create a plan that no one else has the confidence to reach for, to identify and seize an opportunity. The good news is that we are seeing historical changes on multiple fronts. People are listening more than ever and are ready to embrace change. Entrepreneurs, business owners, corporate executives, and everyone in between seem to feel the need to shape something better than what they have now.

Simply being innovative isn't enough to succeed. Entrepreneurs and business owners must adapt and accept disruption to find the positive. To seize opportunities for change in their businesses, the next step is breaking through the preset comfort zones that people set for themselves. Many people are fine with creating some level of change or disruption in their businesses, up until the first point of resistance and then they hit the brakes. This is the upper reaches of their comfort zone and going beyond it is a step too far.

One example is a small business attempting to scale up, to reach a new level in income and service for their customers. With a small management team in place, they may be used to doing all the tasks on their own, while also maintaining control over all aspects of the business. However, with a larger scale comes new challenges and added responsibilities, including the need for a new layer of management and employees to help service the growth. The tough tasks can begin when the original leadership team is forced to give up control to the new layer of management, because they can no longer do it all on their own. Embracing change means roles will be redefined, direct reports might change, and new ideas and processes will flow into the business.

Small businesses might face questions, such as the following, during this restructuring:

1. What changes can we expect to see?

2. What roles need to be changed, updated, or even eliminated?

3. What direction does the information flow? Who has access?

4. Can the existing team grow into this new space and be maintained, or is there a need to build a new, fully functioning culture?

5. Can they embrace the disruption knowing it could mean a huge win for the company?

The answer is that for many small businesses and entrepreneurs, they simply can't handle that amount of change. Ultimately, without close evaluation, change may cause the demise of their business.

Disrupting Ourselves

Personal disruption is another way to radically change yourself and your business. Disruption is a leadership journey; any growth in the company is due to growth individually, by the team, and by the organization.

The best leaders are the ones who acknowledge that they are on a continuous leadership journey, constantly learning and growing. They put themselves into situations where they are pushing their comfort zone; they are going out on the ledge and staying there, even though it's scary and uncomfortable. It's also common that those edgy leaders never feel they've mastered being outside their comfort zones because they are continuously pushing, and the line in the sand keeps moving.

These high-performing leaders always thrust themselves into new and often uncomfortable experiences, knowing that the rewards will outweigh the downsides. These leaders are seeking out coaching, collaborating with other leaders on the edge, and crafting a safe space where they can all talk and explore these uncomfortable spaces together.

Staying out on the ledge is a crucial and essential step in the growth and leadership of any entrepreneur, otherwise, you risk languishing there instead of challenging the status quo. Unless these leaders are being careful to keep growing and pushing their boundaries, they risk not being able to keep up with the changes of their businesses and ultimately failing.

Long-Term Visions for the Future and Mastering Disruption Go Hand in Hand

Businesses work best under timeframes. However, traditional long-term plans don't allow much wiggle room and tend not to be very disruptive either.

So, how can we plan strategically in a way that works and allows us to be innovative and create disruption? Ultimately, we need to strive toward plans that serve the core values and goals of the organization.

I believe strategic success comes with dividing longer-term visions into shorter, eighteen-month increments and focusing on creating a highly detailed plan. I love using scenarios for this exercise because it allows you to plan for pretty much every possible action or outcome, and prepares you for what comes down the pike.

The seven steps to create a rolling eighteen-month plan for success:

1. Ascertain what the goals of the business or company are for the next eighteen months.

2. Devise scenarios that consider the possibility that the world will evolve and impact your business in the next eighteen months.

3. Be as detailed as possible with your business scenarios. Create a strategy to cope with all the possible outcomes. It may be intense, but don't skip this step!

4. Find the common factor(s) between all the scenarios you listed in Step 3.

5. Use the commonalities to create a detailed plan. The first month should be just as fleshed out as month eighteen.

6. Continue to add to the plan by extending the timelines as you roll through, repeating this exercise quarterly—or however often it feels manageable—to stay on track and on course.

7. Review and re-evaluate the plan by asking questions like, "Are we still on track?" or, "Is this where we want to be in eighteen months?" Reflect on your strengths and weaknesses: "Has the past quarter changed our trajectory for the next quarter?" and, "What updates need to be made?" are great questions to reflect on progress.

I recommend entrepreneurs and leaders seek out a variety of possible outcomes and anticipate different scenarios. Such an unpredictable world will surely evolve. It's an excellent idea to create detailed plans on how the business will react, what it will do, and how it will maneuver for the best possible outcome. In the end, your business should end up with a robust strategy for each of these scenarios.

The next step is taking the common factor across them and using that to inform your eighteen-month plan. This is achieved by splitting your strategy into six quarters that you have figured out, with as much relevant detail as necessary to succeed. The caveat is that the last month of the cycle will be as detailed as the first or second month.

The best entrepreneurs and companies have detailed plans for all eighteen months because they have a specific outcome in mind. This level of detail ensures they will get there. Most entrepreneurs and companies struggle with this because looking so detailed, so far in advance sounds like a lot of work.

A colleague recently shared with me that they spoke to the CEO of a software company, who confided that they struggle with strategic planning. Without a plan in place, they are constantly putting out fires and missing the mark on projections. The absurdity is that they have a great product, they know the product they want to build, and what they want to achieve but cannot devise a plan to get there. Continuing on this route, it is unlikely they would ever hit any of their goals or scale.

Conscious Decision Making and Embracing Disruption in the Workplace

I spoke with an entrepreneur who is a fantastic leader, and he shared that he too has an eighteen-month rolling plan for his business. What's even more amazing is that he's constantly '*Mad Men Modifying*' the plan. He asks for input from his coworkers across the organization on a regular basis, and uses that feedback to modify their plans. As a strong leader, he is open to all ideas, scenarios, and outcomes. He uses disruption and being out on the ledge of discomfort to his advantage. He does not hoard the decision-making power from his employees; rather, he empowers them to be part of the process by giving them ownership of their ideas and the outcomes.

What impresses me is that he has done the mental work along with embracing disruption and an evolving strategy. He's constantly in touch with his teams, asking the right questions. And his lead-in? He always reminds his team that this is their plan, not just his. It's everyone's plan and they have just as much right to add or modify it as he does. He consistently empowers his team to participate fully in the process of disruption, which in turn keeps the plan fluid and functional.

I checked in on him again after our initial call to find that his eighteen-month plan had changed immensely. When I asked him why there had been so much movement, he said he was made aware of an opportunity that hadn't been identified during the initial process of building the plan, a scenario they hadn't planned for. When they saw that things were beginning to change around them in that very direction, they were able to make a smooth switch, which turned out to benefit them greatly. Since they had a responsive strategic plan that could flex with change, they could quickly seize the disruption as an opportunity.

It doesn't matter if you own a business, are the CEO or founder of a major company, or run a mom-and-pop shop, the goal remains the same; make conscious decisions while building a strategy and remain pliable enough to receive input, make changes, and update as you go.

Where to Begin with Conscious Disruption

I have 10 rules that make up my process for deliberate disruption. This list is a good primer on where to start being intentional with strategy and disruption.

Rule 1: Lead through relationship

Rule 2: Start with the future in mind

Rule 3: Recognize the power shift

Rule 4: Build openness and trust

Rule 5: Embrace healthy conflict

Rule 6: Scale leadership with agency

Rule 7: Overcome the resistance to change

Rule 8: Leverage digital to grow relationships

Rule 9: Replace perfection with excellence

Rule 10: Embrace the contradiction of order and change

Rule 1: Lead through relationship

Excellent leaders who can manipulate disruption have a whole set of soft skills that differ from their counterparts. Think about the greatest leader you've ever worked with. What were their qualities? What made you enjoy working with them? Ask employees and you'll find that the common theme is that people love working with leaders who aspire to create change while inspiring people to follow them. Feeling heard and validated as an asset to the organization certainly builds better relationships than handing out transactional perks such as bonuses and extra days off.

Perpetual change requires new rules for leaders; it's no longer a top-down or command-and-control approach. Instead, leaders should see themselves as guides, and stewards of the grand vision. Handing over control to those who can successfully execute plans is in the company's best interest.

Rule 2: Start with the future in mind

What will the landscape look like in the next five years? Ten years? What will your customers need later and how will you deliver it to them? These questions need answers *now* so that you are ready when the market shifts. This is where the planning comes into play. Planning for all the possible outcomes means you'll be prepared to shift and ride the wave as it happens, instead of struggling for air after the wave passes over your head.

Rule 3: Recognize the power shift

Being disruptive means addressing the elephant in the room; that's the shifting power dynamic that inevitably is created by disruption. Whereas the seat of power in organizations was once only found in the C-suite and the only decision-makers were those in the corner offices, that's now no longer the case. A top-down decision culture doesn't connect with the way society operates anymore. And truthfully, that's a good thing.

Connection is the new source of power. With most employees viewing and participating in various social platforms, and spending countless hours sharing, commenting, and producing content meant to inspire and connect, they see firsthand the ability to create disruption and break the status quo.

Social media is, by nature, a means of engagement, of testing out ideas, a proving ground for breakthroughs, and a way to voice (sometimes strong) opinions. From Gen X to Gen Z and beyond, it's now the norm to question the dogma of the "old guard" and push for change. It's been 3 decades since the first real social media platform was launched; that's 30 years of disruption, transformation, and chipping away at the fabric of how our societies once stood.

The result is, as you can guess, that corporations and companies who want to stay successful in today's economy and social climate can no longer have one figure at the top calling all the shots with total autonomy and essentially acting as an autocratic leader.

With the advent and growth of social media, a broadening divide in socio-economic levels, and a heightened distrust for how things "used to be done", disruption is here to stay. And the future success of organizations depends on how quickly they adapt and become adept at incorporating disruption into the fabric of their company culture.

And while there might be some resistance by some leaders towards a culture shift of embracing disruption, the new goal of the company leader(s) should be to encourage a comfortable transition for both managers and employees.

Rule 4: Build openness and trust

You'd be shocked at how deep mistrust can be rooted in any organization. Employees who have had their ideas shut down for years will seek validation. Creating an open culture that employees can trust means being transparent and creating accountability.

Trust can be earned through staff check-ins. Listen to and validate concerns, and then take actionable measures! Addressing problems as they come up fosters more trust than you might think. You'll see how this one step can alter an employee's perception of the company, of their leaders, and even each other.

Rule 5: Embrace healthy conflict

There will be conflict—it goes hand in hand with disruption. You're tearing down the status quo and asking people to break out of learned habits. It's not going to be easy, but healthy conflict is crucial.

Overcome the awkwardness of giving feedback. Approach conflict with the belief that everyone has the best of intentions at heart, rather than avoidance and resentment. Consider the power of being able to disagree and then commit to a decision. Directness, when done right, can strengthen and deepen relationships instead of creating alienation and mistrust.

Rule 6: Scale leadership with agency

Agency is the ability to directly impact the most important things and to own decisions. If you want to scale your leadership, especially while creating disruptive change, agency is a necessity. It all begins with shifting the mindset of decision-makers from gatekeepers to facilitators and devising a structure and clear guidelines that help define the limit.

The leader's role is to make sure there is support in place to encourage and validate the agency as employees continue to develop it. There will inevitably be pushback or a shift in confidence as employees test out this new way of approaching their roles.

Rule 7: Overcome the resistance to change

Overcoming resistance is one of the most emotionally difficult hurdles for companies. This is where the majority of push-back lies; hostility to change is extremely difficult to manage and it's not uncommon to feel overwhelmed or even embarrassed. Often this is where companies get hung up. We naturally resist change because we don't know how to deal with uncertainty. It's a very real, deep-rooted emotion. To mitigate it, you can set goals and reward employees when they shift their mindset. Objectives and Key Results (OKRs) are a powerful way to set audacious goals with the full knowledge that you won't always hit them. And that's ok!

Rule 8: Leverage digital to grow relationships

What does it mean to extend and scale your leadership into digital and virtual spaces? How can it benefit you in the long term? It's not about the technology you use but the relationships you can further develop. It's about honing the abilities to listen, care, share, and be more engaging. This means sharing the stories that will align people around common goals and objectives.

Rule 9: Replace perfection with excellence

Many leaders freeze from the fear of failure and believe they must be perfect or suffer the consequences. But that's the wrong way to look at it. Leading disruption requires moving from perfect to focusing on being excellent. Excellence is the opposite of perfection because zero errors mean you're not learning. How can you do this? Try setting impossible deadlines to spur action, and encourage the confidence in your teams to make decisions without all the data in hand. Get out of the habit of thinking that more time to mull over decisions makes better decisions because that's only one way of looking at success.

Rule 10: Embrace the contradiction of order and change

As humans, we crave order—it makes us feel comfortable and it's very predictable, but things can become static. We also crave change, but change can feel chaotic and exhausting. Disruptive organizations and their leaders can find balance and thrive by imposing order and discipline around the process of change. For example, Amazon has a process for creating change using a one-page press release from the future and a six-page FAQ document. Change won't happen unless you have the order—the structure, process, and procedures—to create a container for it.

Here are 3 questions I ask every client as they begin to hone in on what their strategy should focus on:

Question 1: "Who is our future customer?" You need total alignment and understanding otherwise your team cannot strive toward a common goal.

Question 2: "What is our strategy to meet the needs of our future customers?" Every organization should be looking at its current processes and plans to make sure they are capable of supporting and serving its current and future clients' needs. And that can drastically change the outlook for your eighteen-month plan.

Question 3: "What is my/our contribution to making that strategy meet those future needs?" This question pulls into focus how each leader approaches success in their role, and what they perceive to be the essential parts of their job.

If you don't know who your future customer is or you don't have a clear strategy of serving your future customer, you risk not having anyone to sell to. If the leader or their employees aren't clear on where they are going, then how are you going to get there? How will you be able to react if and when things change?

I always start with these questions because when you can create that level of alignment, it will strengthen the core. This gives everyone clarity and expectations of their roles to get to the end goal; then you make executing that strategy effortless.

Company Culture Cultivates an Environment for Disruption and Innovation

When working with different clients I observe how productive an organization can be and how much disruption they can tolerate. They may have all the plans and strategies in place for incredible change and growth. They can even have an eighteen-month goal strategy in place. If the company culture doesn't allow for cross-communication, open-door policies, or a structure that allows review and revision from every corner of the organization, then it will be exceedingly hard to succeed.

The teams that are successfully disrupting their sector completely trust each other. They know the chain of communication and prioritize clearing everything with each other. There is little to no dysfunction in these teams, nothing left unsaid, and tremendous integrity in communication and every interaction. And until you can do that and be crystal clear with each other, you will continue to struggle, along with your strategy.

One of the best ways to create trust is to foster a culture of gratitude and openness in organizations. For one, this type of open environment keeps everyone grounded. When people inevitably struggle with the feelings disruption causes, it's gratitude that can remind everyone why they are on this path. Creating a safe place to feel gratitude empowers teams and leaders to trust one another and peel away the layers of, potentially, decades of siloing and compartmentalizing the organization.

Imagine if you start each meeting with everyone in the room sharing one thing they are grateful for, business-related or not. How would that change the feeling in the room? How would that encourage connection and go against a potential culture of entitlement? Teams of all sizes work better together when they ditch the WIIFM (*what's in it for me?*) attitude and dial up the volume of gratitude.

How Digital Transformation Creates Disruptive Progress

Technological advancement, by its very nature, creates a lot of disruption. Digital change is a form of disruption because it takes a historically analog process and digitizes it. A simple example is going from collecting signatures by hand for a petition to now being able to gather signatures electronically.

Another great example to come out of positive digital disruption is chatbots. You no longer need to call a customer service line, wait on hold, or attempt to speak to an automated service to get support. You can skip that process entirely and interact with a chatbot, a digital customer service AI, which allows you to share your concerns or research answers to frequently asked questions faster than ever before.

Both examples show how information gatekeepers are quickly replaced, roles are adjusted or even eliminated, and paths to information are made easier to access.

Digital transformation can bring about a lot of change within a short period of time. The disruption comes out of the lack of familiarity and can even impact the relationships we have inside and outside our companies.

If you work hard on mastering the relationship aspect of your business, you can minimize the level of disruption that digital transformation creates. If you can link the necessary changes back to your values and determine how they support your desired culture, you can reconfigure meaningful relationships accordingly. With the level of trust you've worked so hard to instill in your relationships, you have the scaffolding in place to weather the turmoil this type of disruption may bring.

Remember: You're Resilient

Not every entrepreneur or business owner will happily skip down the path toward disruption. It's a wild concept that creates a tailwind many people can't fathom or are too scared to face. Resistance will always occur, especially to those who have internalized their pain and discomfort and have based their identity on the inability to change. Creating change in your business starts with you, regardless of whether you're the founder or on a team reporting upward in your organization.

We have seen a shift as COVID-19 completely altered the traditional office setting. No one could predict that entire buildings full of staff would shut down and go remote, rely on video conferencing to hold meetings, and collaborate on digital platforms to conduct complex business without ever being face-to-face. It was unheard of even in the digital age, up until we were forced to embrace it.

Restaurants that relied on putting patrons into seats pivoted to a curbside pickup model with online ordering to stay afloat. We saw the growth of digital attractions, virtual vacations, and a boom in gardening and home renovations. The pandemic forced us to make changes we never thought possible, and it demonstrated that we're more resilient, adaptable, and capable than we may have thought. Resistance to change is deeply rooted in the desire to keep things the same, often because we *think* it's easier. But the pandemic proved that the new normal includes constant change and that those resistant to change are likely to be left behind.

As restrictions ease, and the push to go back to in-person business increases, we're seeing the continuing wave of disruption. The Great Resignation is yet another example of disruption. It's hard to comprehend how we will ever go back to the way we were with the rate of change being exponentially faster.

It's beautiful to see the mindset shift in a willing CEO or founder—to see them apply new management styles as a response to the challenges ahead of them. Many are now shedding old skin, confronting disruption instead of recoiling against it. There is so much opportunity to be had by inviting disruption into your business.

About Charlene Li

Charlene is an expert on digital transformation strategy and disruptive leadership. She has authored six books, including the *New York Times* bestseller, *Open Leadership*, and the critically acclaimed book, *Groundswell*. Her latest book, *The Disruption Mindset*, lays out a blueprint for disruption. She is the Chief Research Officer at PA Consulting and Senior Fellow at Altimeter. Charlene is a graduate of Harvard College and Harvard Business School and a sought-after keynote speaker.

Website: www.charleneli.com

LinkedIn: www.linkedin.com/in/charleneli/

Six Components to Build a High-Performance Culture

Terry Jackson

We all know that leadership dictates culture. The people at the top of any company or organization set the tone for their employees.

That seems simple enough, but it can be tricky to quantify how that works. It begs the following questions: How deeply rooted is the symbiosis between management, leadership, and corporate culture? Is it possible to separate the two, and if not, how can you ensure that you get the results you expect from your team?

The truth is that good management and leadership teams not only set the bar for corporate culture but also exist to facilitate it. Whether it's direction, financing, or planning, a leadership team must choose the right people and give them the necessary tools to get the job done well.

To follow are six core components that any leader can leverage to their benefit to achieve the high-performance culture they want: Purpose, Value, Behaviors, Recognition, Rituals, and Cues.

Purpose

Human beings are always searching for purpose. Many successful personal development coaches talk about the significance of your *why*. It is one of the most important driving forces of a human's behavior.

It's not only modern-day life coaches who talk about purpose and it's by no means a new concept. Napoleon Hill wrote one of the most prevalent books about success in 1937, with a personal purpose being one of the things he recognized as a necessity to succeed.

Hill's view on purpose was that "There is one quality which one must possess to win, and that is definiteness of purpose, the knowledge of what one wants, and a burning desire to possess it."[24] It follows that the human need for purpose is neither new,

89

nor isolated to a single group. In fact, most job satisfaction studies list purpose and meaning very high up on their list of must-haves.[25]

People need to feel that they are doing something meaningful in their jobs, and if they don't, they will likely feel unmotivated and disengaged. But how do you create purpose at work?

What Is Purpose in a Corporate Environment?

Some people define their purpose, at work, as purely earning a living. There's a good chance those people find bigger dreams and purpose outside of the workplace—if not for them, then almost certainly relating to their personal lives and those in it. So, you could say that their primary goal at work is to earn enough to make a living, their purpose being to give their family a better life.

They want to know that the company they work for is doing something worthwhile, even for profit. They want to know that your products and services are beneficial to people and that their role in the company is part of delivering those products and services.

People want to know that their role is necessary and will not become obsolete. They also need certainty that they can access training and support to grow their career, and that there's potential to climb up the ladder.

Purpose is what motivates people to get out of bed in the morning. It's what makes us keep working on problems; we know that solving them, and overall success, will make us feel better. We need to know that we are appreciated and valued.

How Can You Ensure That Employees Have Purpose?

Human beings feel like they have a purpose when what they do has meaning to someone else. This means that your employees should understand what their job is and how it fits into the bigger picture, within your company.

It's often helpful to have flowcharts and organizational charts that your employees can refer to. It's integral that they can see who relies on them for information and support, and to get their jobs done. It's equally important to listen when your team has ideas. If those ideas have merit and can improve the operation of your organization, allocate a space for employees to experiment.

Remaining in control of your role and responsibilities while being able to implement your ideas is a big part of defining meaning and purpose. It's natural for employees to seek validation that they are needed and fill an essential role in your company. When possible, ensure that they know they are a part of a team that serves a purpose.

Setting and Sharing Group Goals

Another essential element of ensuring your employees understand their purpose is to ensure that they understand your corporate goals. Very often, people below upper management aren't entirely sure what your business is working towards. It's almost impossible to score when you don't know where the goalposts are!

While you don't have to share your corporate plans in detail, giving everyone broad strokes of your short-, medium-, and long-term goals is good for clarity and transparency. Communication with department heads and supervisors offers the opportunity to share company visions with their team and help them understand how they are part of the plan.

Values

It's quite popular to post your corporate vision, mission, and values on the walls of your office or on your website. However, when it comes to corporate values, it's a lot more about what you *do* than what you *say*.

Even if you list values like integrity, honesty, trust and service as your corporate values, if your leadership and management team doesn't embody those values, no one in the building will buy into them. Persuasion is achieved through action, in a nutshell, talk is cheap. If you're going to share values with your employees, make sure that they are qualities you really believe in and embody.

Why Do Corporate Values Matter?

When starting a business, most people have a vision for what they want to accomplish. There are objectives that matter, which are not entirely about making money or dominating their industry. These elements can become your company values.

When your business begins to grow, it's easy to communicate those values to the people you work with because of the small scale. However, as your organization gets bigger, there might be several degrees of separation between you and the people who keep the cogs of the company turning.

Over time and through growth, it becomes increasingly challenging to communicate your values to your team. Maintaining your values is an ongoing process. It will give you direction to refer to when deciding who to hire and promote. It will also help you make business decisions. If you can ensure that your employees can define your values and apply them daily, it will ensure that your customers continue to get what they expect from you.

Bringing Culture to Life

One of the biggest challenges with maintaining the values that your company was built on, as it grows, is to ensure employees know what is expected of them. Their responsibilities must reflect and bolster the values in their day-to-day business inter-actions. While you might have communicated these values easily when you were all working closely together, it becomes difficult as your company increases from dozens to hundreds of employees.

As cumbersome as it might seem, you really need to find a way to weave your values into your operational procedures and policies. If you say that customer service is one of your values, ensure that your procedures reflect that. For example, set the precedent for employees to respond to calls and emails within one business day. Provide customer service training to all front-line employees. Empower sales teams to create solutions for your customers when they need to.

At the same time, you need to ensure that your employees always see you embodying those values too. If you say that integrity and honesty are core values, but you keep promoting dishonest or unethical people, your employees will either think you're not really committed to those things or that you're unaware of what's going on in your own business. Neither of those is an impression to impart on your employees.

Values are what you believe. Culture is what you do. The two should always match, or you will need to adapt one.

Can Values Change?

As your business grows and changes, so will you. Things that you might have thought were critical ten or twenty years ago might be less important or relevant in the present. You may even discover something new that matters to you more; after all, views change.

It's okay to change your values as you grow and change. In fact, it's a good idea to take some time every year to examine your personal missions, visions, and values, and make the necessary adjustments. It doesn't matter what your values are.

What matters is that you remain aligned with what you believe in, and what you say matches your actions.

Behaviors

Humans are naturally a highly observant species. We can see that as babies go from crawling to walking and talking within a few short months. Human beings are fantastic at observing others and imitating what they see. It's how we learn, and we never lose this skill.

If you think you can operate by the expression *do as I say, not as I do*, you'll be sure to have some unpleasant surprises. Whether you like it or not, optics matter. Your employees are always watching you, and they will learn to follow the example you set.

If you're ruthlessly competitive and reward people who are the same, your employees will see that as the best path to success. If you don't bother to learn employee names and opt not to show interest in them, those employees will find it hard to be loyal to you and your company.

The way you behave and how you carry yourself has a significant impact on your office dynamics. Make sure you present a desirable set of behaviors for your employees to refer to and follow.

You Don't Always Have to Be Right

One of the most common problems that leaders face is that they believe they always need to be correct. The opposite is true.

Your people will respect you more if you admit that you don't know everything. It also proves that you have excellent business acumen. The role of a leader is to hire the most innovative and qualified people to take on vital roles within the business.

If you are humble and can admit your faults, your employees will feel comfortable doing the same. That will lead to a harmonious and collaborative workplace, which is an excellent reflection of your leadership skills.

Your Employees Should Never Work Harder Than You Do

Company owners and management often tell employees that hard work will get them to the top of the ladder. Management also periodically arrives late, leaves early, and takes three-week vacations every quarter.

It's important to remember that no one will ever be as committed and dedicated to your company as you are. Nor should they. After all, when your company posts record profits, or a large competitor acquires you, you will reap the reward—not your employees.

It's pertinent that you do not ask your employees to work harder than you. Unless it's essential, you should never require or encourage employees to sacrifice their personal time for your company. Your employees will respect you more if you respect their personal lives.

Recognition

One forestry team's biggest challenge is growing trees in a previously established, flourishing forest. The reason is that the branches which form the canopy block the light from the forest floor. So any newly planted trees have less access to light than the established trees. Businesses are a lot like these established forests. Often, we forget that the people who have been around for a long time and are already successful might be hogging the sunlight, making it difficult for others to grow. As a leader, it's your job to understand this and make sure that people whose careers are not as established yet also get recognition to stay motivated and continue to achieve new heights.

People work harder when they know their work will be recognized. It was true in school, when people knew they would get As on their papers and then admission to great colleges, they put in more work. It works on sales teams when top performers get bonuses and perks. It works with everyone else too.

People want to know that you not only recognize their contributions but that you appreciate them. The best way to do that is to tell them that you appreciate their work, and if they regularly go above and beyond, to recognize their efforts through action.

Recognition Should Be Relevant and Valuable

Having an employee of the month program and putting pictures on the wall in your office is a great start to recognizing people, but it's not enough. When you recognize and reward people for their work, it needs to be relevant and valuable to them. Your compensation could be financial, in the form of commissions, bonuses, or raises, or even prestigious, like a promotion or a new office.

The critical thing to remember is that when you recognize people for their hard work or great ideas, they know their work is worthwhile. Since we work to earn a living and to forge a career, that kind of recognition is what we all want. Even if you're not writing bonus checks all the time, offering successful employees special training, or new projects and challenges, is a great way to show your appreciation.

Once again, it's all about what you do, not what you say.

It Should Be Appropriate for the Achievement

Sometimes, simply mentioning someone's hard work during a company meeting or putting a blurb in your company newsletter is enough to recognize achievements. However, if you have an employee who is consistently knocking it out of the park and pivotal to their department and your company, you need to do more. While no one wants to think that they have to buy loyalty, you can be sure that if you're not paying attention to the rockstars, your competitors will be. It's only a matter of time before someone notices your top achievers, and if you aren't paying attention, you will lose them.

Rituals

In Japan, corporate employees stand alongside their desks every morning, listening to their company song, much like a national anthem. It's just another corporate ritual that helps employees connect with the company they work for in creative ways.

Of course, we don't find it crucial that you write a company song, but creating these kinds of corporate traditions and extending this sense of commonality can strengthen bonds between teams and employees.

The better your employees get along, the better they will be able to collaborate. Rituals help boost morality and ensure that things get done to the best of your collective ability.

From Casual Fridays to Company Retreats

There are several ways that you can build rituals into your corporate operations. They don't all have to be a big deal, and they don't have to happen all the time.

One way that many companies build rapport and camaraderie among employees is to have casual Fridays. The idea is that people in casual clothes will be more relaxed, at ease, and likely to engage with others. That helps to strengthen relationships.

Holding events such as company picnics, barbecues, and team-building days are another great opportunity to create rituals while bringing people outside of the office. These activities also help your employees feel more connected to your culture, while often improving communication. Moreover, offering top achievers the opportunity to attend employee events or company retreats will welcome them to work on building relationships with colleagues. Even starting a company softball team is an excellent way to make your employees feel more connected to each other, as well as your company. After all, feeling a sense of belonging is pertinent to showing you recognize employees as humans, not just numbers on a spreadsheet.

Meeting Rituals

Another way to get more out of your team is to create rituals at your team meetings. Having a fixed process and format for your meetings helps to ensure that everyone knows what to expect, and that meetings can be handled faster and more efficiently.

If your team knows that there will be a question period at the end of the meeting, they won't waste time asking questions beforehand. If they know the meeting will run through departments in a fixed order, they will know how to prepare accordingly. If you choose to offer snacks and beverages at your meetings as one of your rituals, you'll also find that employees are much more excited to attend!

Personal Rituals

Perhaps one of the most powerful types of rituals you can create in your company is the personal one, which can be more sentimental.

Some companies choose to buy cakes for their employees on their birthdays. In others, the tradition is the reverse, to bring a cake for the office on your birthday. Many companies have fun traditions that they only use around the holidays, or when someone retires or moves on from the company.

When corporate rituals offer a personal touch, and target one person or a small group, they make people feel appreciated, seen, and valued, which is always good for positive workplace culture.

Cues

According to those in the know, when Queen Elizabeth II stopped eating, everyone else stopped eating too. There is very little chance that any of us ever witnessed that in person, but it's a good example of a cue from leadership. She didn't have to say anything—yet it triggered a response. She simply did something that everyone recognizes, and they all followed suit.

There are many signals you can incorporate in the workplace, including nonverbal cues, which will benefit your team and communication efforts.[26]

Be Consistent

In many companies, accounting and finance departments are very busy during the last week of every month. Often, the accountants and CFOs of those companies will close their office doors during that week, giving everyone an unspoken signal that they should not be disturbed.

If you want to start implementing cues like this, the first thing is to strive for consistency. If you do the same thing every time you are working on a specific type of project or at a specific time of day, people will start to recognize your signals subconsciously, and act accordingly.

Think Outside of the Box

One of the most common challenges leaders face in a post-pandemic world is the fact that we're not all working in the same place, at the same time. It's easy to give your team cues when you are all in the same office, but it becomes more complex when working from home or on a hybrid cycle.

Instead of relying on more visual cues to steer your team in the right direction, consider setting up a series of automated emails to remind your team what their priorities should be, and regarding any important goings-on in your company.

There are some great online collaboration tools, such as Slack and Asana, with virtual workspace options for communication. Many of these tools allow individuals to set their status. This way, everyone on the team knows what coworkers are working on, while understanding when and how to contact their teammates.

Cues from Customers

An essential type of cue your team needs to keep in mind is the cues customers give. Customers won't always tell you their wants and needs directly, but they will often show you by behaving or speaking in an indicative way. Learning to watch for cues in body language and speech patterns is a great way to satisfy customers, and serve them with the products and services they need from your team.

It would benefit your business to teach your team different cues they may receive from clients, along with how to interpret and engage with them. Empower your employees to step outside of standard procedures when they need to, to deliver what customers need.

Adapting Your Leadership Style in a Post-Pandemic World

There has been a growing sense of unease among many business leaders over the past couple of years. When the pandemic made remote work the rule rather than the exception, many had hoped it wouldn't last too long. Many managers and business owners were hoping to spend a few months at home and then get back to business as usual.

Over two years later, that shift hasn't happened, and many teams are still working entirely or mostly remotely, with no fixed end date. As time goes on, more employees continue to adjust, deciding that they prefer working this way. And it grows increasingly harder to convince employees to return to the office. Perhaps the answer is not trying to convince anyone, but changing how you operate to fit into the new normal.

Changing the Way You See Work

The changes that the pandemic has brought to the workplace have been no less momentous and are comparable to those seen during the Industrial Revolution. There is no doubt that business and the workplace have shifted forever. But change doesn't have to have a negative connotation, even if it's uncomfortable; it's important to be adaptable.

It means you need to change how you think about work and employees. Instead of counting how many hours your people are in the office and equating that to their work ethic or efficiency, you need to start measuring results. That may sound ludicrous, but perhaps that's how it always should have been.

Does it matter how long one is in the office or is it more so about the results they deliver? Try to find new ways to give your employees goals and base your performance assessments on how well they deliver on those goals.

There's a common saying, *adapt or die*. One of the most challenging things companies may need to adapt to right now is that remote work is one of the most desirable work situations for employees everywhere.[27]

Most, at one point or another, have said that they will consider quitting if they are forced to return to the office. Well over 90 percent of all employees surveyed in various studies have said that remote work is their number one job requirement.[28] This means that if you don't embrace changes, you are likely to lose part of your existing team. You also risk potentially facing a tough time hiring quality candidates to replace them.

However, it's not all bad news. Remote work has opened new possibilities, like building a global team. When you work remotely, borders and time zones don't matter as much. If you don't find the skills you need in your city, you can expand your search to the rest of the country, or even the world.

Be Wary of Corporate "Spying"

Several companies have faced work-from-home situations and turned to technology for assistance. Some businesses have gone as far as to use software that tracks mouse movements or allows remote access to employees' computers at any time of day, without requesting access. While, as an employer, you might feel more secure that your employees are working when they should be, it also risks destroying a previously established mutual trust.

Employees often interpret this as being spied on, and no one wants to think that the company they work for doesn't trust them. Tracking your employees so closely should never be your first choice of action to measure productivity. If it is, your hiring processes and policies might be at fault.

Look for the Positive

One of the biggest time thieves in a traditional office has always been meetings. It can be quite a hassle to get everyone into the boardroom and to engage in some idle chit-chat while waiting for the meeting to kick off. These meetings often drag on because of in-person arguments or disagreements.

If there's one thing the pandemic has given us, it's an insight into how many meetings are actually necessary. Many teams have been surprised about how much they can get done without a long, in-person meeting. Short online meet-ups between only essential people, as well as emails, and cloud-based software have allowed us to get more done with far fewer meetings. Even if we all end up back in the office, large, long-winded meetings will hopefully remain a thing of the past.

The Buck Stops Here

While many leaders and managers blame their teams for not delivering results, ultimately, that may also indicate a leadership failure. As a leader, it's up to you to set the policies and tone for the company.

You must find ways to continuously motivate your employees, keep them engaged, and help them build a collaborative and supportive team. If those things are not firmly established, or you're stuck in a toxic loop of office politics or revolving door staff turnover, it may be time to change how you operate.

In any company, you get out what you put in, and when you're a leader, it's not only about how much you work. You need to model the kind of behavior you want from your team because they will almost certainly mimic what you do, and not what you say.

About Terry Jackson

Terry is an executive advisor, speaker, and organizational consultant. He is a member of the prestigious Marshall Goldsmith *100 Coaches* and was chosen by Thinkers50 as a Top 50 Leader in Executive Coaching. *CIO Review Magazine* named Terry's consulting company, JCG Consulting Group, one of the "Top 10 Most Promising Leadership Development Solution Providers 2019."

Terry has authored *Co-Creation Leadership: Helping Leaders Develop Their SuperPower of Co-Creation for The Greater Good of the Organization* and *Transformational Thinking: The First Step Toward Individual and Organizational Greatness*. He has contributed to articles in *Forbes, Chief Executive Magazine*, and has authored more than 150 articles on LinkedIn.

Website: www.jcgconsultinggroup.com

LinkedIn: www.linkedin.com/in/terence-jackson-ph-d-57618410/

CHAPTER

6

Creating an Impact Culture

Angela R. Howard

Let's kick off this chapter with a call to action to humbly ground us in the immense responsibility we have as entrepreneurs and business owners:

> *Our actions and choices have the power to create change and positively influence society, as well as entire generations to come.*

These actions, decisions, and choices are rooted in what makes you, you—your values, your impact, your purpose, and the legacy you'd like to leave on the world. *So, how will you leave the world?*

In this chapter, we will focus on the intersection of modern leadership, work, and how to shape a congruent culture for your business, keeping in sight the impact and legacy you'd like to make. We'll aim to shift the mindset that *doing well* and *doing good* are mutually exclusive because business owners and entrepreneurs often focus heavily on the former of the two. *Doing well*, often characterized as achieving the goals and objectives of the company, is actually about the people who are getting the work done. At the same time, *doing good* spans far beyond workplace perks and keeping your employees satisfied. It includes things like:

1. Contributing to your employees' and customers' wellbeing, wealth, legacy, and purpose.

2. Developing policies and programs that correspond with your values.

3. Unpacking and understanding your organization's culture can impact how work does or doesn't get done.

4. Creating sustainable business practices that are efficient and socially responsible to the planet, people, and profit.

5. Understanding your organization or team's impact on the communities you live, work, and serve in.

6. Seeing your business as a container for enrichment to send happier, healthier humans back into their respective societies and communities.

7. Determining your organization's or team's role in social justice issues and ending long-standing systemic problems.

This chapter might be something you read and consciously walk through as you evolve. It's important to understand that your impact as a leader and your organization's impact are connected. It's easy to see "future of work" trends as just that—trends that feel far removed from the reality you're most comfortable with, but the future of work is *here*. We'll review three main global work themes (*The Transformation Trifecta*) that you should be paying attention to. Here's what you can expect to achieve and whom you'll impact with the foundational part of this chapter.

First, impact starts with you. The careers we take on, the communities we build, and the organizations we create are a living, operating legacy of our own. And we're happier, healthier, and more fulfilled as the gap narrows between what we're designed to do and what we aspire to do. Creating awareness and eliminating cognitive dissonance with the impact we want to make is the beginning of building a leadership legacy. We'll discuss *Leadership Mentality* and why this is a significant, modern deviation from what we have taught or have learned about leadership.

Second, your employees: like you, your employees are most passionate when they can work on things that align with their values and identity. The need for a purpose for all humans is potent. It drives engagement, happiness, and performance. Identity and connection to social causes are essential to attract and retain top emerging talent. For example, emerging generations, such as Generation Z, are becoming more impact-driven. They are paying attention to societal and humanitarian challenges now more than ever and are very interested in understanding how they are affected. They expect workplaces and leadership to lead by using their resources and platform to drive broader social change at a deeper level. As we have seen in movements like *The Great Resignation*, the gap is getting smaller for organizations to make clear, coherent, and intentional impacts on cultures. These impacts will allow employees to feel connected to something they are passionate about.

Third, your customers: it's important to articulate and consistently put time, energy, and actions towards a well-defined purpose—*your why*. Your company's vision, mission, and values allow you to make space and prioritize business engagement that fuels your legacy and organizational identity.

Fourth, for society: connecting your purpose to a mission outside of your organization has the power to create change, potentially raising awareness for larger movements of change. Clarifying your impact and acting on it can make work more sustainable for your employees and set an example for other businesses. By aligning social responsibility and leadership, your organization can have a sizable impact.

The Transformation Trifecta Is Driving the Future of Work

Your next thought might be, "*Well, Angela—I know that creating a culture that is conscious and sustainable is the right thing to do, but what's the business case? How do I explain this to my board, partners, co-founder, or members of my executive team?*" The short answer is that the world of work is changing and transforming right before our eyes, and now is the time to think differently.

We're recovering from a global pandemic; we have an aging workforce, *baby boomers*, and an emerging workforce of Gen Z. Digital transformation has accelerated faster than we could have imagined, and has made working from anywhere virtually limitless.

The next generation of work and leadership is here, and if you pay attention to workplace and work-life trends, you're probably overwhelmed with a myriad of data, perspectives, and information about the future of work and leadership. I've distilled these pivotal changes into three main global themes, which I call *The Transformation Trifecta*, which includes interconnected themes surrounding The Great Resignation, an aging and emerging workforce, and the rise of conscious business.

The Great Resignation

The Great Resignation is also referred to as *The Great Attrition* or *The Great Evaluation*. Many unique factors have collided in building up to this perfect storm, including a global pandemic, the reimagining of work and life, and a changing social contract between employees and employers. These factors coming to the surface, all at once, have called for a re-evaluation of what we want and should expect from a workplace experience. With a growing gig economy, emerging workforce, and evolving social contracts of what talent expects of leadership, 41 percent of workers are considering leaving or changing jobs. Navigating forward requires a new mindset and flexibility around how we manage, develop, and create mobility for talent.

The empowerment pendulum is shifting. An energized dialogue is emerging concerning the impact of leadership and work on the masses. The bottom line is that employees are increasingly refusing to settle for tired leadership tropes, passionless leaders, and systemic barriers to success. Progressive workplaces aren't just offering perks—they're challenging minds and hearts and redefining what *work* really means, forcing shifting attention onto overhauling tired leadership paradigms.

This shift is creating positive momentum for society, humanity, and sustainability, and is also causing business owners to face challenges that may not have been previously addressed including:

1. The inability to attract and retain top talent. Competitors are paying more and offering better employee experiences; the familiar traditional workplace cultures and practices are struggling to keep up.

2. Keeping current employees happy, challenged, and fulfilled. It's no longer acceptable to just *survive* in a job. Employees are looking for overflowing cups and environments where they can thrive.

3. Creating flexible work structures that don't limit employees from doing what they're best at. Employees are finding better and more diverse ways to stay productive and connected to the workplace.

4. Compounding years, decades, and centuries of ineffective leadership is catching up with organizations that have not invested in people, culture, and leadership.

Many of these challenges point back to the quality of leadership, making leadership a mirror of culture and directly impacting the work climate. Ineffective leaders continue to be a primary cause of toxic culture and employee turnover—50 percent of it to be exact.

So, how does all of this connect to The Great Resignation? There is now data pointing us to believe that ineffective and toxic cultures have fueled this movement, which demands pushback from employees. In an MIT Sloan article, authors Sull, Sull & Zweig analyzed the impact of more than 170 cultural topics on employee attrition between April 2021 and September 2021.[29] Culture is ten times more likely to contribute to attrition than compensation. The article mentions that "the leading elements contributing to toxic cultures include failure to promote diversity, equity, and inclusion; workers feeling disrespected; and unethical behavior." There is a clear finger being pointed at workplaces that don't care about their employees.

The employer-employee relationship is changing. Limiting engagement tactics to blanket solutions is no longer enough. Many organizations are scrambling to understand what it will take to keep their talented team members. The companies that can attract and retain talent will focus on equity and fairness versus equality. This means a shift towards more listening to employees' needs, as well as personalized and diverse employee experiences with empathetic leaders.

An Aging and Emerging Workforce

An aging workforce, which includes a large population of baby boomers preparing for retirement, and the rapid pace of disruption, has created a widening skills shortage. McKinsey & Company claim that the value of talent and learning programs will equate to the ability to actively identify and build future-proof organizational capabilities, assess existing knowledge and skill gaps, and re-skill teams to close gaps. Many of these gaps center around leadership skills. No change, no mindset shift, and no transformation can occur if leaders lack the skill to build a more inclusive and sustainable workplace.

DDI is a company that publishes a global leadership forecast each year and surveys leaders and organizations across the world. They surveyed more than 15,000 leaders, 2,000 HR professionals, and 200 organizational leaders across industries, levels, race, gender, and other cross-sections of demographics to identify the most critical leadership skills for the future of the workplace.

In 2021, the survey highlighted that only 28 percent of leaders are developing in any one of these critical areas:

1. Driving inclusion, leading across generations
2. Building talent
3. Managing change
4. Digital acumen
5. Strategic thinking and influencing.[30]

This information points us to a concerning trend—a growing gap in building influential leaders to implement sustainable and healthy workplace cultures. This is a giant red flag and a risk trigger for action. If you are not developing yourself and the leaders at your organization, now is the time to double down on this investment.

Social Responsibility and Conscious Business

This recent trend has been a mounting priority for a growing workforce that now includes millennials and Gen Z. Expectations have been elevated and sit on the original premise that organizations have a responsibility to consider how they impact social, humanitarian, and environmental issues. Like the survey and report on leadership run by DDI, Deloitte runs a review on emerging generations. The message this year is clear—the growing emerging workforce has a robust accountability-focused mindset on business' involvement in societal and humanitarian issues.[31] This includes mental health, environmental issues, societal disparities, and discrimination. The importance of justice, equity, inclusion, and diversity will be crucial to fold into our business strategies. The answer to the question *"What does your business stand for and how do you show up?"* is not only nice to have, but also a must-have.

You may have already noticed the intimate connection between social responsibility and conscious business. They are a call to shake up the traditional workplace. What we have done in the past will not work today—nor should it. If we want to attract and retain diverse talent, and create workplaces that are equitable, we must lead the charge as role models.

It Starts with You

If you are a current business owner, the connections may be clear. You may have reached a stage where you look beyond profit as a measure of success, but you may be unsure of how to ignite change. Or you may be a budding entrepreneur or leader in the early stages of building a business or community. There is no better way to spend your time and investment than understanding how your leadership will impact your organizational culture, and community. The next part of this chapter will focus on *you*— and how to implement a focus on people, the planet, and profit into your business structure.

The Science Behind Purpose

The link between identity and purpose is fundamental to the human experience. It taps into a basic need for a shared experience that, when channeled in a positive and healthy way, can create massive momentum and change in your life.

The good news is that most people feel like they have a purpose. Individual or organizational purpose is at the core of your *why* and is an overarching mentality that tends to guide your actions. The breadth and fluidity of purpose cannot be taken for granted. The way purpose is defined here is not equated to "this is what I was born to do" but rather, "this is the impact I intend to make." And the actions behind the purpose may change over time—as we learn, grow, and eventually bring a sharper point to our purpose.

A sense of identity includes characteristics that help us organize, consolidate, and bring our purpose to fruition. To do this, we must consider tapping into elements of the human experience that are fluid, non-binary, multi-hyphenated, and complex. According to McKinsey & Company, 85 percent of individuals feel like they have purpose, but only 65 percent of them feel like they can articulate what that purpose is.[32] This is where fine-tuning elements of our individuality and leadership identity will be important.

Awareness of identity is a cornerstone for building inclusive cultures and fostering a sense of belonging in the spaces you create. Although your identity will undoubtedly drive the issues you connect to, healthy action around identity and purpose is inclusive, not exclusive. Being purpose-driven does not necessarily mean setting out on a narrow and well-laid path. There are diverse ways and opportunities which may offer an array of possibilities that are driven by individual identity and purpose—including your individual leadership styles.

The Leadership Mentality: A Cornerstone of Responsibility and Purpose

When you read the word leadership, you may think of a specific person, persona, or profile. Or perhaps you have a series of lived experiences that have defined good and bad leadership for you. Many think of leadership as a position, a name on an organizational chart, or the person in charge. However, there is a rapidly evolving understanding that the next generation of leadership is motivated by identity, purpose, humility, and responsibility to others rather than power, position, and authority.

In a modern workplace, thinking of a *leader* as the person in charge is missing the last piece of the puzzle. Leadership—the state of mind and mentality, has little to do with the position held and more to do with the impact made, service to others, and positive influence.

It starts with internal awareness and the courage to reflect, iterate, and improve. Jim Collins describes the concept as a step-by-step approach to successfully become a Level 5 Leader. This leadership persona emerged as a key player in transforming organizations from "good" to "great." This level of leadership is a balance—a yin and yang of sorts—of personal humility and professional will.[33] In other words, a leader needs to be modest and vulnerable enough to admit when they are wrong. Seeing yourself as a life-long learner demonstrating an unwavering resolve to improve and progress is also necessary. This is an essential balance for any leader to maintain while looking to see leadership mentality flourish.

A fundamental part of leadership is inspiring a group of people to achieve a common goal. It's *how* a leader motivates others towards accomplishments where the discussion of *good* or *bad* management comes into play. For example, leaders have used force, fear, and intimidation to reach a state of influence, power, or results. This is a toxic way to tear down organizational culture, break trust, and undermine entire teams— leading to short-term effects through fear or manipulation, with long-term damage to people, the organization, and any possibility of sustainable results.

Compare this to the leader who uses inspiration, inclusion, and empowerment to achieve a common goal. The difference between these two strategies is the mentality of the leader.

Empathetic leadership offers better outcomes, more innovation, more engagement, increased retention, and better holistic wellness outcomes.

Leadership mentality is about the mindset and sense of responsibility you portray to others coming along with you. With a new definition of literal and physical workplaces, leading virtually or in a hybrid work environment only elevates the need for effective leadership to actively create a sense of belonging and build community. Key leadership characteristics such as empathy, clarity, and the ability to build relationships have never been more important.

Remember: we can all lead regardless of position or where we sit on an organizational chart. The future of leadership is communal, humble, and focused on community and inclusion—not as an exclusive outdated workplace experience. The next generation of talent expects a more elevated version of leadership than we've seen before, which we believe will evolve into a leadership mentality.

To learn about your leadership impact before you move on, reflect, and answer these questions:

1. What impact do you want to have on others?
2. How are you showing up as a leader?
3. What are you doing well? How are your behaviors positively impacting others?
4. What could you work on to improve your leadership behaviors? (Tip: talk to 2-3 people for external input)
5. Think about a team you have led. How can you be in service to them? How can you remove barriers?
6. Where might there be opportunities to give your team additional empowerment and ownership over their work?
7. What structures have you established to ensure your team feels supported and connected?

8. What do you know about your team as people? (motivations, aspirations, and challenges)?

9. How are you creating psychological safety, and enabling people to feel safe enough to speak up and be authentically themselves in the spaces you lead?

10. In what communities do you have influence? What opportunities do you have to build community, and increase belonging and positive change in your sphere of influence?

Let's Talk Culture

Now that we have a solid understanding of how culture can impact our business and how leaders can impact culture, let's talk about how to create a culture of influence. We can't talk about a culture of impact without unpacking what *culture* is. At its core, culture is just a consolidation of habits and micro habits over time. It shows up as:

• Observable behaviors

• Consistent behaviors over time

• The way you make decisions

• What you tolerate and what you don't tolerate

I often talk about the word "culture" with a lowercase and "Culture" with an uppercase, as they differ in definition. Given my background in workplace and organizational psychology, most of my perspectives are from the vantage point of company culture (lowercase), but we can't dissect and unpack culture at an organizational level without understanding the many layers of the social elements of Culture (uppercase) that exist and influence actions, behaviors, and social norms. Societal culture and workplace culture form a complex web that we need to understand to start the ripple of change.

Both *culture* and *Culture* are similar in the following ways:

They are perpetuated and modeled by dominant forces (leaders or influence) who seek to change or preserve their integrity.

They both occur organically and systematically at the same time.

Social norms are set and assumed, and the terms of engagement are subconsciously created over time. Disruption to these terms is often met with resistance. They may go unquestioned for years or even generations.

There are "in groups" and "out groups" created based on the dominant traditions.

Changes are both a movement and a disruptor simultaneously.

Movements to drive change are a force of their own. Making an impact and a lasting change is both an art and science.

Workplace Culture: What Is It?

Building a culture within an organization is commonly referred to as a *soft strategy*, and in recent years has emerged as a key business tactic. According to a Gallup article, "Rich company cultures and commitments to employee happiness both have a direct relationship with shareholder returns. Culture-conscious companies rise above industry benchmarks, and they out-earn and outperform their competition."[34]

Commitment and effort are needed to proactively keep a pulse on how organizational purpose, vision, values, and behaviors bring people together for success. Pulse checks are underrated, and sometimes underutilized tasks—especially during times of change and transformation. Culture is the heartbeat of any organization's strategy and touches every part. Every organization has a culture, and many organizational leaders have an aspirational culture in mind. Many businesses invest resources in changing culture without understanding their current culture and what areas they need to impact to instill change. Remember, culture is a culmination of consistent actions, behaviors, and rituals that drives how work gets done. In a workplace, prioritizing how work gets done is the special sauce for any organization. It's possible to replicate products and services, as almost every company has a competitor. However, your culture, including your people, bring a competitive edge because they cannot be copied.

You are likely participating in and reinforcing culture without even knowing it. This is because you are also likely reacting to the standards and norms in which culture you are operating. Over time those actions become normalized and internalized—even if they are toxic or detrimental to the organization, the employees, or the people the organization ultimately serves.

What Culture Is Not

Organizations worldwide are in a frantic and frazzled state of *start and stop* because they are blind to what factors can have an impact on culture. Opportunity for cultural impact and change is left on the table—and the loss of impact is massive. Aimless activities and unfocused energy can create a tremendous amount of waste, frustration, and harm to an organization.

Contrary to popular belief, culture is not a program, perk, or offering. Culture change and transformation can often become nothing more than a marketing plan. Organizations lean on complexity and communications surrounding why a culture program is different when they should start with opportunities to change habits in a micro manner over time and then celebrate what has changed for the better along the way. This is how change occurs, not through a massive transformation roll-out, flashy launch dates, or buzzwords to describe your culture initiative.

Organizations are often confused when they hire a Head of People (or similar titles) and don't experience the magical change and return on investment that they expect. Culture is not an HR initiative. Resourcing a single team or person with a responsibility that only leadership can role model, reinforce, and hold others accountable for can quickly turn a well-intended business decision into a tragic loss for all parties involved.

Lastly, culture is not performative. There's nothing more damaging to your culture's impact than a mismatch between words and actions. Fostering an environment with a focus on positive impact is a lifelong journey for your business. You can never take your eye off culture because self-actualization can take decades to build but be reduced to a mindset of scarcity and lack of abundance within days due to performative actions. Culture decay is the deterioration of a group's traditions and values over time. You can probably imagine that self-actualization equates to the full potential of both the individual, and the organization, while also including the potential impact that may result. Culture decay occurs when your organization's ability to satisfy part of the basic needs of your employees, your customers, or the communities you impact is compromised.

Full Circle: A Call to Action

By now, you hopefully have a solid understanding of why the topic of leadership and sustainable business practices is an important cornerstone of your business. Hopefully, your internal questioning has shifted from *why* to *how*.

Here are five actionable items that you can take away from this chapter and begin implementing:

1. Articulate what statement your individual leadership impact should make to people and the planet. Do the same for your organization or business.

2. Invest in an executive coach and impact-aligned leadership development program for your leadership community.

3. Hold bad leaders accountable. The positive results they produce for you in the short term do not outweigh what their negative impact will cause in the long run; don't risk compromising your impact, your employees' lives, your customers' lives, and your pocketbook.

4. Ask for feedback from your team and look for input on how they would describe the culture of your company. Don't be afraid to look in the mirror and face some hard truths. Act on any incongruencies you hear and always report on progress—taking no action after asking your employees' opinions can create more damage than good.

5. Focus on equity versus equality to make a meaningful difference to your employee and customer experience.

These actions will take investment; they will take time, and they will take your commitment. But the impact these action items can make on your business, your employees, and the world will live on with your legacy and years to come.

About Angela R. Howard

Angela is an organizational psychologist and culture impact strategist working to build human-centric workplaces, better leaders, and thriving communities alongside growth-minded leaders. She works with leaders to diagnose symptoms of harmful culture, challenge objectivity in the face of hard truths, and facilitate meaningful changes in organizations through operationalizing culture-building.

Before starting her own company, Angela has served in leadership-level talent management, employee experience, organizational development, and executive Chief People Officer (CHRO) roles for various organizations. Her podcast, Social Responsibility at Work, focuses on how human-centric workplaces can create stronger communities and societies.

Website: www.angelarhoward.com

LinkedIn: www.linkedin.com/in/arosehoward/

How to Make Conflict Resolution Easier and More Productive

Jerry Fu

When I became the manager of a new pharmacy, I needed to find teammates to help run it. The most convenient solution was to hire people I knew from my previous employer. This previous pharmacy had just folded, leaving all its staff desperate for work. To give myself the best chance to succeed, I immediately recruited one of the lead technicians, who we'll call 'Lisa.' While I didn't work directly with her, she always seemed knowledgeable and competent. Given how little time I had to get a team ready for my first day, I didn't evaluate Lisa or other potential candidates beyond their titles and my previous interactions with them. I onboarded Lisa as soon as I was able.

After a month of work, Lisa began showing troublesome behaviors. Primarily, she liked to sow discord and doubt among the team, even as she acted like everyone's best friend. Whenever Lisa made mistakes, she would deflect any concerns I expressed. Everyone on the team, including myself, became reluctant to confront her because of her belligerence. Reluctance led to resentment. My hesitation in taking stronger measures to address her bad work habits took days, weeks, and even months. Every morning I would go to work with a pit in my stomach, wondering if Lisa would be in a good enough mood to get her tasks done without additional negative impact. I didn't want to feel like I had made a mistake by hiring Lisa. But the evidence against her kept mounting.

After the pharmacy had been open for about a year and a half, an incident with a patient occurred. Fixing the error required spending a lot of money. After further investigation, we traced the mistake back to Lisa's miscommunication. I knew I had let her poor job performance go on for too long without taking stronger disciplinary action. My bosses and I took her aside to discuss the situation. Her continual resistance to own up to any part of the situation led us to write her up.

Irritated, Lisa immediately stirred up more dissension among our team. Another incident occurred with a different technician, Emily. Her error was addressed in a conducive manner with the entire team, leaving her name out for anonymity. However, Lisa then convinced Emily that management had false motives for addressing the situation with the whole team. When management found out what Lisa had done in response to her writeup, they finally dismissed her.

Looking back, the emotional toll of unresolved conflict Lisa brought onto the team grew each day we left it unaddressed. In response, a system to address situations like this more promptly was developed at our workplace.

With the right mindset and approach, you can feel more confident in handling conflicts like these, and identify and address them early on to prevent consequences from escalating.

The Cost of Unresolved Conflict Is Massive

Avoiding conflict altogether is a sign of artificial harmony. Conflict must be constructive and reach an ideal balance. This is the point where conflict is as far away from artificial harmony as possible, and at the same time not yet destructive. Conflict, when we can manipulate it to our advantage, can be like striking gold. Organizations that embrace positive conflict as a tool to find the best way forward tap into the potential of more people, create more balance and alignment, and achieve better results.[35]

Research shows that 85 percent of employees deal with conflict of some kind, while 29 percent deal with conflict frequently or always. Also, 64 percent of employees have experienced a toxic personality in their current work environments, and 94 percent of workers have known someone like that in their careers. The average number of hours spent per week on workplace conflict in a nine-country survey ranged from 0.9 to 3.3 hours, with the

United States averaging 2.8 hours. Unresolved conflict increases absenteeism and employee turnover rates. Together with the additional cost, the financial impact of the amount of time lost to conflict in the United States alone is an estimated $359 billion according to one study.[36]

At worst, an unresolved work conflict leads to company closures due to losing clients, revenue, and employees. At best, it leaves you with an uneasy stalemate. People work to avoid getting fired instead of giving their best efforts. Eventually, they stop settling for subpar work environments and quit. Companies with healthy cultures have a turnover rate of approximately 14 percent, which increases to almost 50 percent for companies with unhealthy cultures.[37] More than ever, companies cannot afford to lose competent employees and tolerate ineffective ones.

To stay viable, employers must equip their employees with the skills to maintain strong relationships with their teams, bosses, and customers. But evidence reveals that few employers are serious about investing in the necessary training. A massive 95 percent of people who received training say a conflict resolution program prepared them to navigate conflict better, which empowered them to seek mutually beneficial outcomes. But the impact only goes so far when 60 percent of employees never receive training in the first place.[38] With the majority of employees not being given the tools to positively engage in conflict in the first place, the workplace is much more difficult to navigate.

The Role of Mindset in Resolving Conflict

Your actions reveal what you believe. The story you tell yourself about conflict determines how you approach it. If you struggle with conflict, evaluate your thoughts about it. Ask yourself not what feels accurate but what is most helpful.

In *Mindset*, Carol Dweck discusses the difference between a fixed and growth mindset. People with a fixed mindset believe a quality like intelligence is an innate trait, unattainable unless you were born with it.[39] In contrast, people with a growth mindset believe qualities such as intelligence can be developed. In order to resolve conflict acceptably, it's important to interpret handling conflict as a skill you can learn instead of an inherent attribute. The framework on how to handle conflict I will provide you with at the end of the chapter won't matter if you don't believe you can use it. If you insist on a fixed view of your ability to handle conflict, you will limit your own success when you engage in conflict with others. To improve yourself, start by evaluating your thoughts.

Many of my personal beliefs in my youth became obsolete, inaccurate, or irrelevant as I grew up. I realized I had a fixed mindset about many skills in life, especially leadership. I believed people were either born with a skill or they weren't—there was no chance for improvement. If I had to put in the effort to get good at something, that meant I didn't have the talent to do it from the start. This felt true for both mental and physical skills, whether imagining a solution or playing an instrument. Resolving conflict was no different. It seemed like a skill that would remain unattainable for me. After a few unsuccessful attempts to navigate difficult conversations, I told myself I would never get any better. Because I didn't believe I could improve, I didn't even bother trying. I gave in every time someone was upset with me. After enough exhaustion and resentment accumulated, I knew I needed to change my approach. But I didn't know where to start.

Limiting thoughts will hinder your path to skill mastery if you don't know how to identify and remove them. As such, self-doubt will undermine any success you achieve, accusing you of being more lucky than good. Permitting yourself to believe you can become competent points you toward success. Once you apply a growth mindset to conflict resolution, you will be surprised at what changes are possible for you.

A Better Way to Think About Conflict

Take some time (yes, now!) to journal your thoughts around conflict and ask yourself how they got there. Factors can include family, work, and any critical experiences while growing up. Compare your notes to the thoughts and examples listed below to see where you are and how you can move forward. Seek out feedback from people you respect once you have your thoughts on paper. Here are some reflection questions to get you started:

1. What do I believe about conflict?
2. Where did those beliefs stem from?
3. How does conflict make me feel?
4. Why do those feelings arise with conflict?

As observed in the examples above, conflict results from a disagreement in expectations or priorities. An organization needs to be able to handle all kinds of conflict, whether healthy or unhealthy. Unhealthy conflict arises when people don't meet expectations, like my situation with Lisa. Eliminating conflict altogether isn't the goal. Successful teams understand the value of healthy conflicts and even encourage them. They have a process in place to discern what kind of conflict they're dealing with and to ensure a constructive approach whenever it arises.

A closer look at these examples reveals the root issue: the people's beliefs about conflict. In companies that sustain major setbacks or go bankrupt, employees see conflict as the barrier to the conformity they seek. Or, they see conflict as a problem to avoid. In success stories, conflict is a catalyst for refining ideas and generating alternative solutions. With the right approach to handling conflict, an organization can change its trajectory to not just survive but thrive.

Whenever you encounter conflict, see it as a call to action. As long as the people involved in the conflict agree on how to engage with each other respectfully, conflict is not something to fear or avoid. Furthermore, conflict can be a blessing. It reveals the real issues people need to address. Once you identify a situation you have to deal with, having an effective system to resolve conflict reduces hesitation to engage with it.

The Top 9 Unhelpful Beliefs on Conflict and What to Replace Them With

The general trends around limiting beliefs fall into two main categories: pessimism about your ability (*Can I do this?*) and pessimism about the situation (*Will this turn out okay?*). To identify and remove limiting beliefs, examine your thoughts, evaluate their accuracy, and replace any negative thoughts with the suggestions to follow:

1. Unhealthy Belief: *I'll never be good at resolving conflict.*

    Replacement: *Anyone can improve at resolving conflict with enough practice.*

James, a friend of mine, had a problem. His roommate, Matt, had defaulted on his lease. James didn't like confrontation, so he tried to ask Matt nicely about either paying up or moving out. Matt assured James he would obtain the necessary funds. However, Matt still hadn't produced any money after two weeks. James didn't want to revisit this conversation. But he found himself resenting Matt more each passing day without any payment.

After seeking advice from his friends, James' next step was to give Matt an ultimatum. He decided Matt had to pay in full within two weeks or move out by the end of the month. Still uncomfortable with having another face-to-face conversation,

James drafted an eviction notice with these terms and taped it to Matt's door.

The following day, Matt begged James for a seven-day extension after reading the notice. He insisted that the terms of the ultimatum were unfair—especially since he lost his job and hadn't found a new one. Knowing that Matt missed a job interview because he fell asleep, Matt's request added to James' frustration. But James didn't want to seem cruel, so he reluctantly granted the extra time. Even with the extension, all Matt had to show for his efforts was to text James with two days left, stating he was working hard on getting the money. By the time the extension ran out, Matt still hadn't provided payment.

James had grown tired of Matt's empty promises. In a moment of clarity, James texted Matt back and told him to use any money he obtained to cover rent costs at his next place of residence. Only then did Matt start packing up his things.

James had trouble confronting previous roommates whenever they left the kitchen or laundry room messy, so he was pessimistic about his ability to deal with Matt. Successfully convincing Matt to do the responsible thing and move out was a big step for James. This happened only after James evaluated each attempt and made appropriate adjustments until he got the result he desired.

Takeaway: conflicts won't resolve themselves, so it's up to James to keep trying until he obtains a resolution. James learned from each attempt. After enough lessons, he eventually got through to Matt, helping him realize that giving James vague hope about payment was not an adequate substitute for actual money.

2. Unhealthy Belief: *Strong relationships never have conflict.*

Replacement: *Conflict happens in every relationship, even in the strongest ones.*

In *Scary Close*, Donald Miller mentions a conversation he had with Paul Young, bestselling author of *The Shack*. Donald always admired Paul's interaction with his wife Kim and six strong, independent grown kids. Donald also appreciated Paul's family for their openness and honesty. When Donald asked Paul about their secret to having such great relationships, Paul disclosed to Donald the affair he had while his kids were young. Forgiveness from each of his family members was a long, arduous process. Fortunately, the family's commitment to reconciling with one another helped them survive Paul's mistake.

Takeaway: you don't see the work that's being done in private to maintain relationships. Conflict may cause relational damage when avoided. But when faced dead-on, it can strengthen relationships. Any married couple can confirm how much work their marriage requires to keep it healthy.

3. Unhealthy Belief: *Resolving conflict involves coercion.*

Replacement: *I don't need to coerce if I collaborate.*

On my second day as a church class director, some difficult news arose. My friend Erica informed me that Nick, a newcomer to our group, was being accused of harassing women in the class. Nick denied causing any trouble when I called him to address this allegation. As long as he was defensive, we couldn't make any progress investigating what was actually going on.

Nick needed to understand he wasn't being attacked. Instead, he was invited to help sort out this situation. If he was innocent, he could identify and clear up any misunderstandings, making sure he didn't offend anyone again. If he was inadvertently causing problems, he could apologize and regain the trust of the group. Otherwise, he would have to leave. Once Nick realized having an open and honest conversation was the best way to resolve things, the class was able to have a more constructive dialogue with him.

4. Unhealthy Belief: *Being open about my frustrations is rude.*

Replacement: *I can be upset without being disrespectful.*

Tina is a friend of mine. She had an uneasy relationship with Steven, her boss. One evening, while she was out for dinner with friends, Tina noticed Steven was trying to call her. Since she was off the clock, she let the call go to voicemail.

The next day at work, Steven berated Tina. He questioned her commitment to the company because she didn't make herself available beyond office hours, no matter how small the request. As long as Steven needed something from her, he thought communicating with him would supersede whatever else she was doing, regardless of the situation.

Steven's outburst angered Tina, and she wanted him to apologize. But she wasn't sure how to get an apology from him without antagonizing him further. As much as she disliked working for him, she couldn't afford to get fired.

Tina navigated the most desired outcome of her next encounter with Steven. She mentioned her desire to be the best employee she could be for him. She wanted his input on how to do that, and she asked for his permission to have a conversation. Then she acknowledged that their working relationship seemed to be in bad shape.

Having acknowledged the state of their relationship, she explained she was occupied when he had called. She then apologized if ignoring his attempt to reach her came across as disrespectful. After expressing her willingness to do her part to repair the relationship, she could finally articulate her request for clearer expectations so she could meet them more effectively.

In short, Tina framed the conversation for Steven's benefit and asked for his help in addressing any problems. This kept Steven from taking her frustrations personally. Even if the conversation felt awkward, it would still be productive.

5. Unhealthy Belief: *Initiating conflict is upsetting, and I don't like upsetting others.*

    Replacement: *I can't stay silent if I truly care about someone else.*

As of 2016, a billion people still resorted to open defecation. This is mostly due to a lack of access to clean water. Open defecation leads to the mass spread of diseases like cholera and roundworm, leading to suffering and death. Organizations like WaterAid thought that building latrines would solve the problem, but their efforts failed. There was insufficient instruction and no awareness of cultural norms. People either didn't know how to use a latrine, or they felt too embarrassed to degrade a clean toilet with their excrement. Building latrines also did nothing to directly confront the uncomfortable truth of open defecation the local people didn't want to admit to, let alone address.

Observing this, Dr. Kumal Kar introduced a new process, Community-Led Total Sanitation. In this process, a facilitator arrives at a village and asks to learn about their sanitation methods. Walking around, he asks for help identifying where people defecate. As the villagers show him around, he discreetly helps them see how feces from open defecation piles get into their water and food supplies, with methods such as flooding from rain or when flies land on their food.[40]

If facilitators are worried about whether the people like them, the problem won't go away. The facilitators care about the people they visit, which is why they bring up the difficult issue. They leave the villagers no choice but to acknowledge and act on the issue.

6. Unhealthy Belief: *I can't drum up enough courage to engage.*

    Replacement: *If courage is lacking, use curiosity instead.*

When I checked the voicemail at work one Friday morning, the first message I listened to was from an angry patient. She paid for her prescription on Tuesday, but the courier service we used had not delivered her medication yet. Worse, the courier seemed to have lied when they notified her while attempting to drop off her prescription. On top of that, the courier's customer service representative was dismissive of her concerns when she called them to address her problem.

The patient also complained to the doctor about her experience with our pharmacy, possibly jeopardizing the good terms we had with the clinic. If the doctor decided to stop sending us prescriptions because he got tired of complaints, the pharmacy could lose too much business to stay viable. High stakes indeed.

If I had been afraid of conflict, I would be tempted to avoid talking to her at all. But that would be unprofessional and bad for business.

Alternatively, what if I just wanted to learn more about the situation and her perspective?

Thinking of the discussion as an opportunity to get as much information as possible, I called her. I explained I wasn't happy with the quality of service from our courier, either. Hearing her out without interruption gave me the chance to show her I was an ally. Having a genuine curiosity for her thoughts diffused the situation. She even thanked me for the way I listened to her.

7. Unhealthy Belief: *I must defend myself when confronted because I don't like others being upset with me.*

    Replacement: *Criticism provides a chance to learn, then improve.*

Evan is a FedEx account manager. He noticed a drop in business from one of his accounts, a pharmacy. He called Jenny, the manager, to find out why. She shared an example to explain why FedEx was now the last resort whenever the pharmacy had to send out packages.

A patient who lived in a rural area was expecting the medications he needed after having surgery. These were urgent because the combination of drugs would reduce pain and prevent possible infections. However, he only received a fraction of them, and the medications to treat his pain were missing. His story was inconsistent with the tracking information for his package, which showed he signed for all of them in person. When Jenny called the customer service department for clarification, the customer service representative told her the delivery person was allowed to use a COVID waiver in place of an actual signature. Not surprisingly, the patient was upset that he didn't receive his pain medications.

When Jenny submitted an appeal to contest the losses, FedEx denied her case. They stated that because they had all the documentation they needed to show they did their job properly, they had no obligation to compensate for the incident.

Jenny's goal wasn't to make Evan feel guilty. But since he wanted to know what was going on, Jenny's best action was honesty. Jenny even gave suggestions on what changes FedEx could make in order to regain her business. As unpleasant as Evan might have felt hearing Jenny's frustration, he knew that Jenny's feedback, and her willingness to share it, would benefit FedEx so they could earn back more business in the future.

8. Unhealthy Belief: *Conflict is uncomfortable.*

   Replacement: *Short-term discomfort is worth the long-term benefit.*

Lisa had a problem. Harry, a guy new to their church group, had asked her out. Even though Lisa already had a boyfriend, she didn't want to disappoint Harry by declining his request, so she gave him her number. She ignored Harry's texts and calls, hoping he would figure out she wasn't interested in him.

However, something worse happened.

At the next gathering, Harry confronted Lisa. Having found out she was already in a relationship, he asked her why she even gave him her phone number. She apologized, admitting that being honest would have been better than leading him on.

In hindsight, Lisa had a legitimate reason to say no to Harry. But her discomfort with the initial conflict of saying no complicated her situation. Telling him upfront that she wasn't single might have felt temporarily awkward. But she could exhale with relief afterward, knowing she wouldn't have to address the situation anymore.

9. Unhealthy Belief: *I'm not sure how to achieve success if I don't know what it looks like.*

   Replacement: *I can always study someone else's success.*

If you struggle with conflict, here are some books you might find helpful:

The Four Conversations, by Jeff and Laurie Ford: Of particular focus is what the authors call a "closure conversation," which helps organizations address broken expectations and restore relationships.

Humble Inquiry, by Edgar Schein: Schein helps readers navigate the tension between being task-oriented and people-oriented. He also shows how showing curiosity and a willingness to learn prevent tension from escalating when dealing with conflict.

Difficult Conversations, by Douglas Stone, Bruce Patton, and Sheila Heen: One of the most useful parts of this book is when the authors provide ways to avoid the most common pitfalls people encounter while they are dealing with conflict.

Instead of thinking:	Replace it with:
1. I'll never be good at resolving conflict.	Anyone can improve at resolving conflict with enough practice.
2. Strong relationships never have conflict.	Conflict happens in every relationship, even in the strongest ones.
3. Resolving conflict involves coercion.	I don't need to coerce if I collaborate.
4. Being open about my frustrations is rude.	I can be upset without being disrespectful.
5. Initiating conflict is upsetting, and I don't like upsetting others.	I can't stay silent if I truly care about someone else.
6. I can't drum up enough courage to engage.	If courage is lacking, use curiosity instead.
7. I must defend myself when confronted because I don't like others being upset with me.	Criticism provides a chance to learn, then improve.
8. Conflict is uncomfortable.	Short-term discomfort is worth the long-term benefit.
9. I'm not sure how to achieve success if I don't know what it looks like.	I can always study someone else's success.

Five Steps to Respond to Conflict

Earlier in the chapter, I hinted at a five-step framework to help you deal with conflict more effectively. Now that you've adapted your thinking around conflict, here is a stepwise approach to respond well to it.

Here are the five steps:

1. Imagine what a successful conversation would sound like.

2. Find ten seconds of courage to reach out (remove your hesitation).

3. Script your critical phrases (remove pessimism about your chances for success).

4. Rehearse your critical moves (remove fear about your ability to execute).

5. Do it (remove pessimism about your process).

The first step to having a successful conversation is as simple as making a gentle request for changed behavior, like asking a roommate to stop leaving unwashed dishes in the sink. Other times, success might mean finding a compromise. Two friends could agree to stay away from controversial subjects in their conversations, like politics or religion. In some situations, a successful conversation means one person telling the other that their relationship needs to end. Allowing for the room and possibility of success precedes achieving it. Having a target in mind for the conversation also keeps it focused on the relevant issue.

Take ten seconds of courage to reach out—remove your hesitation. Get over the hurdle of initiating the conversation, even if you're not feeling brave. This can involve calling the person, sending an email, or texting the person. Doing this quickly keeps you from rationalizing why you don't want to have the difficult and necessary conversation. This action also keeps you from backtracking once you've set things in motion.

It helps to map out or script your critical phrases. Eliminate pessimism from your outlook for success. Jot down the topics you want to cover and the case you want to make. Anticipate possible pushback from others, then draft your responses to the rebuttals. Once your thoughts are on paper, you can organize them into a logical flow. Ideas that stay in your head might be forgotten. This may help boost your confidence. Think of your notes as a guideline, rather than a literal script.

Remove your fear about your ability to confront or execute by rehearsing your critical moves. Practicing beforehand allows you to fail without fatal consequences. Failing in a safe environment removes embarrassment as well. Observe your body language and tone of voice in a mirror at home, making sure you come across as calm and confident. Involve role-playing with friends to make sure you don't trip over your own words during the actual conversation.

Finally, remove pessimism from your work ethic. The cost of inaction is usually higher than the risk of trying and failing. Having results you can evaluate is the first step toward improving. Following through with difficult conversations separates the doers from the dreamers.

Failure is not fatal when dealing with difficult conversations. Start by viewing conflict as a helpful and productive opportunity. Then have a robust system in place to make resolving conflict easier. The goal is not to avoid or remove conflict altogether, but to make sure we allow space for it in a way that strengthens relationships and organizations.

About Jerry Fu

Jerry is the founder of Adapting Leaders. Embracing the struggle of leadership saved his pharmacy career after he got fired. He has facilitated leadership workshops for over ten years, and he got certified in leadership coaching through the International Coaching Federation (ICF). He also holds certifications in Emotional Intelligence (EQi) and Talent Optimization. He has presented for professional organizations like the Phi Lambda Sigma Pharmacy Leadership Society and the Organization of Chinese Americans. He has a heart for developing Asian-American leaders the way he wishes he had been equipped growing up and is excited to help them deal with leadership challenges more effectively.

Website: www.adaptingleaders.com

LinkedIn: www.linkedin.com/in/jerry-e-fu-pharmd-acc-53710187/

Self-Care: The Secret Sauce for Leading a Fulfilling Life and Successful Business

To follow is a typical conversation at the start of a coaching conversation, or an after-work meeting.

"How are you?"

"Good! Everything's great! How are you?"

"Good, thanks. You look a bit tired. How are you really doing, my friend?"

"Yes, I'm so exhausted."

"What's making you feel that way?"

"I have so much going on in my business right now! There's just not enough hours in a day to get everything done. . ."

"How do you feel about that?"

"I'm ok, don't worry, I just need to power through these
    coming weeks, and things will calm down. . . I'll be fine."

If I had a dollar for every time I had a conversation like this;
full of toxic positivity, linking our self-worth to success in business, and external factors pressuring us to be on top of things.
These are three of the most prominent reasons why business
owners, leaders, and entrepreneurs would rather say 'I got this'
than admit that they need help. When we remain in this stage for
too long, we risk losing our identity while neglecting our
individual needs.

Entrepreneurship is not for everyone, and it comes with
more than just a strong commitment. It comes with a price tag:
financial pressure, high customer demands, and expectations
from employees, to name a few. Everything in your business
eventually becomes *your* problem. Neglecting our own needs for
rest and keeping a healthy balance in life, while aiming to build
companies to fulfill a dream can sometimes cause more
nightmares.

To put it bluntly: no, you won't always be fine. Powering
through and hoping for a less stressful phase ahead is little more
than a pipedream. Likely, new urgencies will arise and keep drain-
ing your energy, and the feeling of being overwhelmed and stressed
will continue to stay in your life—potentially worsening over time.

That's why this book's third theme is about self-regulating
and self-care. While our previous themes have taught us skills
and capabilities that focus outward, we must now direct our
attention inward. The leading topics are self-awareness, mindset
shifts, and preparing ourselves first, before we set out to lead
others and a business.

Leading a business is not as glamorous as the few hyper-
successful entrepreneurs or social media can lead us to believe.

Mostly, it is hard work. Yes, it can also be incredibly fulfilling—if you choose a field that heavily overlaps with your passion, and if you bring the right people with you. Still, leadership and entrepreneurship can feel like an uphill battle. That's why leadership advisor Tony Martignetti talks about climbing the right mountain—the one that works for you. In his chapter, he helps us embrace the importance of self-care, and shares his secrets to become *battle-ready*. He describes the advantage of humility-based leadership and how it links to authenticity (i.e., leading a business based on who you are).

To figure out who we are we must allow ourselves to embrace the intersection of intellect and emotional intelligence in relation to what we want in life. Teresa Quinlan, a certified coach and expert on emotional intelligence, helps us regain life balance by figuring out what is meaningful to us and what sparks happiness. She shows us ways to master EQ as a way to self-actualize, and practice self-care. One of the benefits is that we avoid big emotions while making big decisions for us that we later regret. This will be of use as I have yet to meet an entrepreneur who hasn't struggled with this at some point in their life.

Knowing our personal preferences, gifts, talents, values, beliefs, purpose, and tendencies is another vital step in leading a self-aware life and successful business. It's a process that consists of quite a few steps. Dr. Ken Keis shows us how personal style connects to our entrepreneurial style. He provides a framework for understanding the self and others. Linking self-awareness to stress, health, and wellness levels, as well as to topics of self-worth and what happens around us, he invites us to explore our whole personality.

I will close this theme with a personal story about an incredibly difficult period in my life. In 2019 and 2020, I realized that I had all the skills I needed to succeed, but something was holding me back. It took me some time to understand that the missing part was linked to how I mentally approached life and business. I describe the mindset shifts that made all the difference for me. Using personal and business-related examples, I offer approaches that will help you reflect on the mindset shifts that enable you to run a more successful and sustainable business. These mindset shifts will contribute to the living legacy you want to create. Hopefully your takeaway will be that achieving success in life is not only a matter of hard work but of other defining factors as well.

Self-Leadership and Leading in Challenging Times

Tony Martignetti

During my time as a finance and business strategy executive in the corporate world, I remember being so worried about getting every detail right in my presentations. I would review them repeatedly until I strained my eyes. I would work endlessly up until the deadline, leaving very little time to prepare myself mentally and answer any questions that may be asked. It became cumbersome and frustrating because I wasted my efforts before the final mile.

This paralysis by analysis is something with which many perfectionists struggle. They often only see the trees and lose sight of the forest. As I progressed into leadership roles, I noticed that this myopic view would not serve me well. I had to shift my mindset and learn to lead myself more effectively if I had any chance of leading a team. I had to find out how to be a leader who doesn't get stuck in the weeds. If I wanted to maintain the energy and vitality to lead others, I had to become more intentional in allocating my time and energy.

What I discovered is the power of self-leadership. Once I stepped into my power as a leader, I started to shape my world, and felt more fulfilled in the process. Whether you lead your team, company, family, or organization, it starts with leading yourself. However, this can be easier said than done. Self-leadership is not something fully achievable, it's more of a development path; to be successful, it requires continuous improvement and adaptability that weaves through life.

For the perfectionists out there, just because the game is not measured in terms of winning or losing doesn't mean it's not worth playing. Effective self-leadership is the power-up you need to stay relevant and up to speed to level up. Embracing self-leadership will unlock many advantages in your life. You will be able to evaluate your strengths and how to leverage them effectively, have clarity of purpose, and take more decisive action.

This will also help you better connect with others, making self-leadership a worthy endeavor!

It starts by taking the journey inside to understand what drives your thoughts, feelings, and actions. This inner journey and the methodology used is what I call *Inside-Out Coaching* because the inner transformation experienced ignites your outer transmission. What you transform inside comes across to people you interact with daily. The journey inside can unearth who you truly are through:

- Taking personal responsibility: Discover what you can control and identify what actions or micro-steps you can take to move forward.

- Uncovering your beliefs: Determine the code you live by. What are the "truths" you have chosen to believe about yourself, others, and the world?

- Revisiting your narrative: Identify the stories you tell yourself about your past, present, and future.

As you take these steps, you will become more self-aware, more emotionally courageous, and ultimately more connected to the unique way you lead. This will only result in more advanced, powerful self-leadership. Then, you can extend this new understanding of how to lead others, both directly and indirectly. The change in becoming accountable for your leadership will begin a ripple effect; how you show up in the world and how you lead yourself is absorbed by others and then spreads outward.

How Does Self-Care Fit into Self-Leadership?

Once you can lead yourself, you can learn to lead others. It's important to remember that you are the one who has to come first. It is not selfish; it is about ensuring you can share your best self and previous expertise with the world around you. As the flight attendant before every flight explains, *you must put your own oxygen mask on first before assisting other passengers*; this is the foundation of self-leadership.

Leadership is caring. In other words, you have to care about people to want to lead them. And so, in some ways, when you think of self-care, it is taking leadership of yourself. You already have to take care of yourself to be there for others. Self-care and care for others are significant parts of self-leadership.

There is a tendency to double down during challenging times, invest more energy in work, and forget to prioritize well-being. This is not sustainable, and when managed, can be avoided. You can't run at full capacity all the time and still have anything left in the tank for yourself or others. So, even during those extreme periods, finding time to recharge is essential, not just physically but mentally, emotionally, and spiritually.

The saying that *slow is fast* is a great way to monitor your self-care. This paradox may be hard to grasp at first, but its truth and necessity eventually become clear. When you slow down and take time to think, you can see a more straightforward path. When discussing this concept with clients, I love sharing a mindfulness acronym, STOP. It is really simple but powerful. STOP stands for:

Stop: Whatever you're doing, pause momentarily.

Take a breath: Reconnect with your breathing. The inhaling and exhaling is an anchor to the present moment.

Observe: Notice what is happening inside you and outside of you? Where has your mind gone? What do you feel? What are you doing?

Proceed: Continue doing what you were doing. Or don't. Use the information gained during this check-in to change the course. Whatever you do, do it mindfully.

Using this practice creates an opportunity to move forward with intention instead of on autopilot, allowing you to make decisions with more clarity. In his book, *Thinking Fast and Slow*, Daniel Kahneman explains our two thinking systems.[41] In *System 1*, we move naturally, working efficiently and automatically. In *System 2*, we slow down and use more effort, but get significantly more powerful results. System 1 is where most people live, and it is like riding a ten-speed bike in first gear. They are pedaling furiously and moving slowly, wasting time and burning energy without realizing it. System 2 is where people who have mastered their goals live. It's like riding that ten-speed bike in eighth gear. They pedal slowly yet consistently, and build speed, momentum, and power.

The impasse stands; by moving slowly, you can significantly speed up. It's counter-intuitive, and most people don't have the fortitude, or the patience required to reap its reward, while the successful players know that it's essential to build their legacy. That's what my goal is with my clients. I help them build the inner strength to move slowly and create something truly extraordinary.

Many people are in a chaotic rush and build castles out of playing cards, which eventually tumble over. However, there is another path to create something that stands the test of time and takes on a life of its own. Unfortunately, self-care is something that we often ignore. We usually take care of our material things, such as our homes and vehicles, before checking in with ourselves. It makes sense because these are significant investments, and we want to ensure they are not neglected. We often forget to prioritize our regular care practice, something more valuable than anything else we could own.

It's essential to create a routine maintenance plan for our mental and physical health. In the context of slow is fast, if you race around the racetrack at top speed for the entire race, at some point your tank may be empty.

You will eventually find yourself broken down on the side of the road, wondering what happened.

Building Capacity Beyond Yourself

Let's shift gears a bit to expand beyond yourself. What does a team need to be able to sustain their ability to move forward, especially in challenging times?

Your team needs to know that they can overcome massive challenges and achieve bold goals together. If the new level of achievement becomes the baseline or the performance expectation, the system will eventually break down. Your team is like an engine. When you run it at full speed without maintenance for too long, it will eventually break down. Your employees are not meant to be running at full capacity at all times. We must continually find ways to slow down, recharge, and be ready for the next challenge. However, managing this necessary recharge does not mean we shouldn't stretch ourselves. There needs to be an understanding of individual capabilities and team expectations. When we overcome significant challenges, we stretch our capacity and see new possibilities. It is critical to return to a lower gear to maintain ourselves and prepare for the future.

Change is like a rushing river that knocks us around and has us in a constant state of high alert, trying to keep our heads above the water. We must be agile enough to adapt without being overwhelmed. Change has always been a factor, but I think now there is a necessity to embody an attitude that embraces change when it comes. Microsoft is probably one of the best examples of facing change headfirst. In 2014, Microsoft suffered an identity crisis and needed to take a new direction forward, when they brought Satya Nadella on as CEO. He shifted the collective mindset of the organization to embrace change and adopt a learning mindset. They had to stop getting stuck in paradigms that were no longer relevant and adapt to the external environment. If a massive organization like Microsoft can embrace change, how about you?

Let's Get Battle-Ready

It is time to get yourself and your team *battle-ready*! I don't mean it literally—it means building capacity so that you can adapt to new challenges. When a team is battle-ready, they have a foundation of trust and safety; they know each other's strengths and blind spots and are ready to face whatever happens next. The key competencies of a battle-ready team go by the acronym REAL, which stands for:

- Resilience: The ability to face adversity and grow as a result. When a team has stability and strength, there is less attachment to the outcome. They know that a lot can happen along the way, and they will have to react accordingly.

- Emotional intelligence: The capacity to be aware of and manage emotions, including effectively developing and managing interpersonal relationships. When a team builds emotional intelligence cohesively, they are attuned to the needs of others and check-in to make sure that everyone is heard and supported.

- Adaptability: The ability to change our ideas or behavior to deal with a new situation or environment. When a team is adaptable, they understand the landscape enough to react calmly in the face of a challenge, even if they don't have all the information.

- Learning agility: This speaks to our capacity to learn. It concerns knowing what to do when you don't know what to do. It's about learning from past experiences and applying them to new situations, adapting to unique circumstances and opportunities.

When you commit to building capacity in these four areas, you will set yourself and your team up for success, especially when facing new challenges. The great thing about these competencies is that they get reinforced through repetition. A team builds resilience through surviving setbacks and learning from failures, which usually require the ability to learn and adapt. Building on adaptability as a group requires emotional awareness and a good understanding of others. From there you can pinpoint where there is a need for more support and whether your team is ready to move forward.

Emotional intelligence is one of the most critical skills we need to develop to be battle-ready. Emotions are the underlying language that explains our actions and reactions. Since we have unique ways of expressing our feelings, we have to look beyond what is on the surface. Words and actions are just one part of communicating with one another. Emotional intelligence is about looking deeper to understand what is driving the members of your team.

These social skills have become essential in the past few years as we have shifted to a virtual work model, and we are not as closely connected as we once were. We need to be increasingly aware of what we say, and how we say it, along with its impact on other people. We also need to be mindful of what is not being said as we look around the room. As leaders and entrepreneurs, we may be anxious to move fast and cover many agenda items to keep up with the pace, but if we slow down and look around, we may realize that we are not connecting with the people we should be. And, as attributed to George Bernard Shaw, "the biggest problem in communication is the illusion that it has taken place."

The Humility Advantage

To prepare our teams for the future, we need to start by admitting that we don't have all the answers. We have to bring some humility into the way we lead. Practicing humility involves showing empathy and respect for others. For many leaders, such humbleness is interpreted as a disadvantage or flaw. It might come across as weak, lacking confidence, or indecisiveness. But this couldn't be further from the truth. I like to see humility through the origin of the word *humus*—which means ground. Humility is a sense of being grounded or calm and measured in your responses. As a result, you remain centered and react without getting flustered or animated. With this groundedness, we can stay open to new perspectives and possibilities. If you see empathy through this modest lens, you can use it to your advantage instead of regarding it as a flaw.

When you combine humility with courage, you have a truly battle-ready leader. Instead of conceding immediately, an appropriate answer would be: I don't have all the answers right now, but I can work with what we have to move us forward, despite the uncertainty and the unknowns. I have seen this often during the COVID-19 pandemic from leaders I have worked with, who oversee successful teams. When their original plans were not working out, they courageously opened up to their teams and collectively reworked their solutions.

I have been working with a CEO at an immuno-oncology therapeutics company. The company's clinical development pipeline challenged her. There were many potential directions to move forward, but the company exhausted its funding options, and they had to place a bet on one indication. She felt pressure to decide on the correct path and didn't want to make the wrong choice or disappoint the team. But, with some humility and courage, she worked directly with the team to decide on the best option together. It may seem counter-intuitive. Why would someone follow me if I don't know the answers? How can my team trust me if I'm not 100 percent confident in the plan? Yet through such humble honesty, the opposite is usually true.

Taking ownership and being honest with your team is at the center of most leadership challenges. Your employees respect and believe in you when you take ownership of your decisions and stick to your word. It takes much courage to be this way, but the impact you have will be powerful. When you stand up and face the truth instead of shifting blame or sweeping things under the rug, you are modeling an example for others to show up this way too. You want the leaders on your team to own their mistakes and realize that it is okay to be wrong—what you do with that realization is essential.

I have found that leaders who try to show up inauthentically or hide the truth are not fooling anyone, especially in the long term. Humans can see through the facade of fake leadership. We know when someone is not being honest or putting on a show. If you are showing up with false images, you may eventually let down your guard and show glimpses of your true self, and that is when it all starts to fall apart. On the other hand, if you lead authentically from the beginning, people will truly see you, and you will resonate with them even more, and that will have them join you on your journey to create a meaningful impact.

One of the most well-known examples of authentic leadership is Bill George, the former chairman and CEO of Medtronic. He wrote the book *Authentic Leadership*, sharing his experiences leading Medtronic during a challenging period of its evolution. His leadership had a lasting impact on the medical device company. According to George, the five traits of an authentic leader are:

- Pursuing purpose with passion
- Practicing solid values
- Leading with heart as well as head

- Establishing connected relationships
- Demonstrating self-discipline.[42]

These are compelling traits that are the foundations for an effective leader. However, one thing that these traits all have in common is that they all require a high level of humility and courage.

The Impact of Your Self-Leadership

The impact of self-leadership beyond your team is something to consider. By being straightforward about who you are and what you want to contribute to the world through self-leadership, you can authentically communicate your desired impact to the world. When you begin to see that your business is driven by an inspired purpose to create a meaningful impact and not just make money, others will see that. When you have a company like this, your customers will want to come on the journey and become tremendous supporters. This is linked to creating a ripple effect that spreads, starting from your company, into your customers' lives and beyond.

In essence, your products or services represent something that is a force of good in the world. And I think that's worth striving for—having a brand that customers are proud to be associated with and promote. When you build this type of open communication within your business, even when you falter, your supporters are usually willing to stick by you and move past minor issues because they believe the brand has good intentions.

A great example of this comes from Chobani, a food company with a mission of making high-quality and nutritious food accessible to more people while elevating communities and making the world healthier. The CEO of Chobani, Hamdi Ulukaya, has created a powerful ripple impact through his strong leadership. Not only did he take care of his employees by paying higher than average wages, but he has actively funded and championed many important causes. Ulukaya and his company have supported initiatives that help refugees worldwide while creating a memorable brand that is reputable as a force of good.

So, does this sound like something worth pursuing? When you start understanding and leading yourself, you can build a foundation for something truly compelling. When you develop the capacity to face challenges and then allow time to recharge, you become truly battle-ready! You can create a meaningful impact on those around you from a place of strength and clarity. And that is a legacy to make you proud.

About Tony Martignetti

Tony is the Chief Inspiration Officer at Inspired Purpose Coaching. He is a trusted leadership advisor, entrepreneur, author, podcast host, and speaker. With over twenty-five years of business and management experience, he elevates and equips leaders with the tools to navigate change and unlock their true potential. He has worked as a finance and strategy executive, collaborating with leading life sciences companies, and running small businesses, including a financial consulting company. Tony is the host of The Virtual Campfire podcast and the author of *Climbing the Right Mountain: Navigating the Journey to An Inspired Life*.

Website: www.inspiredpurposecoach.com

LinkedIn: www.linkedin.com/in/tonymartignett1/

9

Creating a Balanced Life That You Love

Teresa Quinlan

Every time someone says the phrase 'work-life balance' I cringe. It's like an invisible button somewhere between my belly button and solar plexus. When it gets pushed by this phrase, my face flushes, my abdominals flex, and my mouth opens. "There's no such thing. It's just life balance because work is part of our life, not separate."

I understand the sentiment of this phrase. The reality for many is that work is inherently unfulfilling—your career can steal a lot of the time and energy from other areas of life that bring more joy. The rest of life gets the scraps, last night's leftovers, minus the 1-minute zap in the microwave. After all, grinding day in and day out at work leaves little time for leisure. And so, it doesn't really feel like work is part of life. It feels more like it's sucking the life out, hence the separation of work from life.

The next level of entrepreneurship is about breaking through this grind and dissatisfaction with one's career and turning it into fulfillment. Perhaps even more so, seek to make entrepreneurship a part of your life as a whole. Seek a life of fulfillment, a balanced life, built by design—not default. In emotional intelligence lies the skill of self-actualization, which is required for self-leadership to be attained. In this chapter, we will explore ways to build a life by design and how not to revert to the default trap.

The Four Emotional Intelligence Skills for Well-being

A quick internet search shows that creating work-life balance lands in the top New Year's resolutions people make, right up there with losing weight, living healthier, stopping smoking, reducing drinking, and finding love. Except people aren't calling it leading a balanced life. They call it spending more time with family, reducing stress, enjoying life to the fullest—or simply: being happy.

In emotional intelligence, monitoring happiness is referred to as well-being. One of the four Emotional Quotient (EQ) skills that contributes to well-being is *self-actualization*. The other three are self-regard, optimism, and interpersonal relationships.[43] These four skills lay a strong foundation for a life by design. Every client I engage with, whether an entrepreneur, business professional, executive in finance or tech or construction, or even a student, has work to do in these four areas.

All emotional intelligence skills have value, which depends on the situation, circumstances, and results desired. In the context of life balance, self-actualization has the greatest impact on outcomes. This is why I focus on self-actualization in this chapter.

As an entrepreneur, self-actualization skill development can pay dividends. In return, it fuels the elusive work-life *balance* quest—your ability to live a rich and enjoyable life both personally and while working. It's possible to lead an extremely fulfilling life, one that you pursue by design rather than by default. After all, being an entrepreneur means you get to call the shots on not only what you want your work to be, but how you want your work to be part of your life. What often happens to entrepreneurs is their work becomes their life. Every piece of it. It consumes their mornings, days, and evenings, both awake and sleeping hours. It consumes their weekdays and their weekends. Losing sight of the balancing aspect means you can say goodbye to vacations and time with the family. Say hello to work, work, work, twenty-four hours a day, seven days a week.

Becoming an entrepreneur happens for many different reasons. For some, it's to get away from the pitfalls of the corporate space. For others, it's to take control of their time and schedule. The fulfillment comes out of bringing something into the world through their zone or spiral of genius. The thing that jazzes them up. With this comes the freedom to choose where and when they work, salaries and expenses, and coworkers. Entrepreneurs have the choice to work on the things that bring joy, to bring something innovative into the world. To be able to make all the decisions for life is essential for balance. To have greater control.

We are feeling beings with the power to think. However, we may prefer to believe we are thinking beings with the capacity to feel. There's a significant difference in rephrasing these statements that warrants our attention at the entry point to discussing the relationship between entrepreneurship and emotional intelligence.

What Is Emotional Intelligence?

Emotional intelligence, or EI, is our ability to interpret our emotions, how we create them, their nuances, as well as how they impact us and those around us. One might find the principles and concepts of EI simple and logical. However, it becomes difficult to demonstrate our emotional intelligence or execute our EQ because our emotions are involved. For each of us, our emotional capacity will be different; in some emotional states, we can be high functioning and high performing, while in others we are low functioning and low performing.

Think of a time when the most difficult emotions in the human arsenal were present in your life: fear, anger, betrayal. How easily could you access your intellect or make a logical decision? It's increasingly difficult to stay calm and centered, to be creative or innovative, or even to solve a difficult problem in a negatively charged emotional state. It's hard for us to think of many times when we were able to have the emotional fortitude and perform at a high level. More often, we can remember the times when we fell to the level of our emotions. We were impulsive. We were foggy-brained. We made bad decisions. We withdrew. We avoided.

Mike is the CEO of a multi-billion-dollar company. He and the executive team have been working together for decades. They all grew up in the same company, most starting from entry-level roles, growing through to management and eventually to the 'third floor' where the executive offices are.

Mike has a habit of blowing up. When he is angry about a particular failure or simple mistake, he uses it as fuel for the blow-up. Mike claims that these blow-ups kick start other people's engines and if he doesn't do it, people get complacent. He told himself that these blow-ups are motivational.

When Mike and I reviewed his EQ 360 assessment, open-ended feedback revealed how his coworkers felt about his behavior. Here are some of his coworkers' reviews:

> "It's abrasive and doesn't feel good at all. I just tune him out."
>
> "It's abrupt and doesn't work the way he thinks. More often I do the exact opposite just to prove a point."
>
> "It's been years that Mike has used the 'blow up' technique to spark motivation in others. We all know about it, so when he does it now, it has little impact. It can seem childish and manipulative. And we all know that's not what he intends. It would be better for him to figure out a way to articulate what he is really feeling and wants rather than keep doing this."

Quickly, Mike discovered that his intentions and the outcome didn't match. He was doing more harm than good, unintentionally de-motivating employees.

By learning to harness his anger and communicate it with intention, Mike was able to clearly highlight the gravity of the situation and pull his people toward the objective rather than push them away. It is vital to be able to develop emotional self-awareness and emotional management skills to focus internally.

Otherwise, our emotions may go as far as grabbing the steering wheel and choosing the radio station, the route, and the temperature.

Not Letting Big Emotions Make the Big Decisions

Next-level entrepreneurs strengthen their emotional intelligence. Especially in challenging situations, they manage emotions like stress, fear, and anxiety in highly proficient ways by applying proactive strategies they developed.

Part of one's ability to separate emotions from hard decisions will involve challenging what we currently think, and what we've been allowing ourselves to experience. Emotional intelligence skills can only develop when we practice them actively. Our awareness of our emotional vocabulary, and how we feel about the sensations we experience daily, is improved by paying acute attention and being objective.

For example, we could take a few weeks to intentionally focus on what we experience happiness around. Track it—a literal 'tick, tick, tick' list in a notebook:

- Dinner with my family
- Conversation with my best friend
- Run with the dog
- Gardening
- Reading a book with a glass of wine
- Backyard BBQ with my friends

When we pay attention, we start to get to know ourselves and how we respond to the life we are leading. We gain insight by evaluating how emotions impact us. And not just happiness—pay attention to what triggers anger, and the varying degrees of negative emotions (including annoyance, irritation, frustration, rage, fear, and anxiousness). Looking under the hood of these emotions, which are secondary to sadness and fear, we can discover the driving factors to many of our emotional disruptions.

When observing internally, I can pinpoint that I am afraid of not being enough, not making enough money, not being smart enough, not being successful enough. *Not enough* is an unhealthy driver in the entrepreneurial world because it leads to impulsive decisions when the stakes are high. When emotions are high, intelligence and self-awareness are unhealthy drivers and may get in the way of success in our entrepreneurial journey.

How Do I Self-Actualize? How Do I Achieve Life Balance?

As a coach, I like to ask big questions, and it's time for one: how can I achieve a work-life balance? Life balance begins with figuring out what is meaningful to you, and then actively seeking out the things that spark happiness; happiness is the indicator that you are in balance.

Grab a piece of paper, or a notebook, or a sticky note, or a napkin, or the envelope from your last piece of snail mail, and something to write with. In the middle, draw a circle and put your name in the circle.

Now, think of a life that you would consider rich and enjoyable. What are all of the things that would be part of your life in this ideal situation? As you are the center of your universe, surround yourself with those things, like the solar system. You are the sun, and these factors that make up your rich and enjoyable life, are the planets. These may be elements that are currently part of your life or need to be in your life in the future.

FIGURE 9.1 Self-Actualization: The Circles Exercise

There isn't an ideal or 'correct' number of orbiting circles. Each person will have a different picture. From this activity, we begin to discover that we might have things in our life that we dedicate time, energy, and resources to that aren't meaningful to us.

There may be some stirring questions to reflect upon. Are there circles populated with things that society, friends, or family impress upon you as being necessary? Are you putting them in your life when you really don't want to or need to? Are you attempting to please others? Are you doing so to avoid arguments or disappointment?

I now permit you to remove the non-meaningful things from your circles, as they steal time, energy, and resources from your life.

If you continue to give time and space to things other people want, you will feel unfulfilled. When we feel unfulfilled, we feel unhappy and disappointed; we tend to be easily triggered by our environment, both internal and external. This can often lead to performing at a low level, not making good decisions, struggling in our relationships, beating ourselves up, and chipping away at our own self-esteem.

When we self-actualize, we clear the clutter to make space for what we value the most. Then we pursue the fulfillment of the things we value most by intentionally cultivating emotions of well-being. This puts us in a high state of functioning, which allows us to perform well. Beautifully, our IQ stays turned on and our decision-making is more crisp, strategic, and tactical. Our ability to say 'yes' and 'no' becomes easier because our intent is focused, which means we've defined what's meaningful to us. In this space, we have a lot of clarity around priorities before our need to make decisions.

What Is Meaningful, Not Just Social Impression or Obligation

Sometimes, asking yourself if something is meaningful to you will lead to an absolute and resounding *YES*. Intuitively I can sense it, emotionally I can feel it, and intellectually I know it. Alignment is essential. Sometimes, we think or hear the *should* and *shouldn't*. It comes from social pressures, peer pressures, or structural pressures that exist. Ultimately, these voices can lead to an 'out of alignment' response; we may have a logical reason for why it should be meaningful or important, but we don't have emotional or intuitive alignment, which usually means it's not essential.

Removing non-essentials from our list of meaningful things is a difficult task. We are forcibly challenging things that, socially, we might feel pressured to strive toward, which are our obligations. For example, when I ask a client to tell me what is meaningful for them to attain a rich and fulfilling life, they have a circle for spouse, family, friends, or kids; however, they usually don't have all of those things at the given time. When probing further, I'd ask, "Why do those things get a circle?", the answer is, "Well, they're supposed to be there." That's when the red flag goes up. According to whom? Is it meaningful to you?

Then we can discuss deciding for ourselves, and how to handle the conversations that spark discomfort. As soon as we remove any circles that weren't put there for them, their emotional well-being increases because the pressure is released, and they no longer need to prioritize those things. It's almost like they've received permission to be authentic, and that permission provides a kind of freedom they weren't experiencing before. They can now accept themselves.

We can perfectly translate these habits to our business as well. With so many things happening at once, such as clients', employees', and the general public's needs and expectations, it's hard to prioritize our own. We may be on social media, watching how others manage their business, and thinking that's how we should be running ours. We do this without asking the probing question, "Is this meaningful to *me*?" We constantly forget to consider if business decisions are aligned with personal desires, goals, values, beliefs, purpose, and desired impact.

The way to the root of what belongs in our circles is with a compassionate inquiry. As we self-discover, we inquire with compassion and curiosity rather than judgments and self-criticism. We ask probing questions including:

- When did I learn that this 'thing' was supposed to be meaningful in life? Why did I learn that?

- How do experiences and lessons from my childhood influence how I make choices now?

- How does this help me? How does this hinder me?

- Do I still believe the same things now?
- If I was to change my beliefs, what might happen?
- What might I lose or gain if I keep the belief?

Compassionate inquiry means we reflect internally without judging our responses. Simply allow them to be. When we let self-discovery lead us, eventually, we ask the question: If I *can* have everything in life, what do I truly *want*? When we design our life with intention, we flourish at our highest capacity. When we do this, the ripple impact is monumental. People see our joy and fulfillment, and we light up rooms when we walk into them. It's infectious, it makes others inquire about how we got there, and it allows us to share our process of self-discovery and self-actualization. We can become a beacon for other people to do the same. In this way, self-actualization is not selfish.

As entrepreneurs, we constantly scrutinize ourselves and look for ways to do and be better. We can be judgmental about ourselves and now I'm asking you, *the next-level entrepreneur*, to turn that switch off. But how do we do this?

Flipping the Switch

First, we have to be able to recognize when the judgment switch is turned on, when we're comparing ourselves to others and focusing on expectations others have. Noticing is the gateway to change. After all, we cannot change something we are unaware of.

Second, when we recognize we are in unhealthy judgment mode, we need to call it out and correct it.

I have a client, Claire, who struggled with a judgmental internal narrative. She would beat up on herself, question her intentions and how people perceived her, and go so far as to question if she was being nice or unkind in various situations. And on and on it went. This made her feel stressed and overwhelmed and often kept her from asserting herself, standing firm in her values, or expressing her needs.

As we worked on building Claire's emotional intelligence, we also worked on how to address the inner critic. In an exercise on quieting the inner critic, Claire first had to give it a persona.

We created Karl, an old white security guard at a bank. He's been working there way too long and all day long you can hear him mumbling under his breath. He has opinions about this person and that person. Once the persona was in place, Claire needed to write back pocket statements to use every time she noticed Karl was present, to silence the inner critic.

"Shhhhh Karl. You're talking nonsense."
"Karl. . .no one invited you here. It's time for you to leave."
"I get it, Karl. You're judgmental and critical. That's not me."

In as quickly as a week, Claire was able to silence the power of her inner critic from disrupting the path she was on. She experienced greater levels of confidence and self-assurance. She stepped up at work for more challenging projects, and eventually earned a new role and a promotion.

Assessing Your Circles

As you look at your needs, you may already recognize that some of your circles are fulfilled—you're knocking it out of the park. Go ahead and give those circles a check mark.

You may also notice that some circles are unfulfilled—they aren't getting the time, energy, and resources they need. You may even feel a lack of wellness stemming from them. Give those circles an 'X.'

Self-actualization is twofold. The first part is understanding how we actively create the life we want. The second part is identifying how we are not.

Choose one of your fulfilled circles and ask yourself this series of questions. Capture your answers.

1. What emotions or feelings do I receive by giving time, energy, and resources to this area of my life?

2. Why is this area of my life important to me?

3. What happens to me when I don't give this area of my life the attention it needs to be fulfilled? How does that negatively impact my well-being?

4. In the past, what have been the things that pull my attention away from this area of my life?

5. How will I ensure that I maintain the importance of this part of my life?

Choose one of your X-marked circles and ask yourself this series of questions. Capture your answers.

1. Why is this area of my life important to me?

2. How do I feel as a result of not giving time, energy, and resources to this area of my life?

3. What emotions would I receive by fulfilling this area of my life?

4. What is one small action, or tweak, I can make to achieve greater fulfillment in this area of my life? When do I want to take that action?

5. How will I hold myself accountable for taking that action?

6. When I dedicate time, energy, and resources to this area of my life, where will I borrow time from?

7. Whom will I impact when I take time from this other area?

8. How will I communicate to them what I am doing and why, so my actions do not negatively impact them?

Our emotions can be incredibly distracting in our business. We can feel fear and let that fear drive our decisions. We can be cruising along feeling confident and competent, and in an instant, an external trigger can bring us to our knees. We're sent into a tailspin. For a business, this can be catastrophic because it ends in potentially rash decision-making and behaviors that quickly sabotage success.

In short, we need meaningful circles to have a high level of decisiveness about our life—all parts of our life—and then we intentionally go after fulfilling the vision. These questions you've explored are part of being decisive and taking wise action aligned with your vision.

Does This Mean We Don't Consider Other People?

There will always be people in our lives whose opinions we value. We want their experience, their advice, their opinions. Learning from others is important because we can glean insights for our own journey. At the start of my entrepreneurial journey, I invited 25 people for coffee who were anywhere from 3 months to 25 years ahead of me with their business goals. Each person was incredibly willing to share the pitfalls, lessons, decisions, and more with me. I took ferocious notes on what was meaningful to me, but I could only do this because I was already aware of what I wanted for my business. I also had a business mentor for four months who helped me identify future potholes. In doing so, I strongly believe I catapulted myself past those potholes and achieved greater success earlier in the journey.

What is most important to this step is balance. We cannot let someone else's opinion override our own, or take priority. That's when we get pushed around and cornered into living life on default.

Blow Up Each Circle and Get Specific

As you explore your circles for life balance over time, consider that you can take any one circle and blow it up. Take the circle and make it your center so that you can look at the components that make up this important area of your life. When you blow it up you can discover the criteria for richness, meaning, and fulfillment.

For example, if 'work' is a circle of meaning for you, you can look at the components that contribute to fulfillment within that area of your life (see Figure 9.2). Then self-assess to which degree it is fulfilled or unfulfilled to inform your actions for balance.

As an entrepreneur, let's assume some of the components for work that add meaning, richness, and fulfillment. Include hours

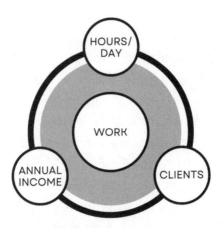

FIGURE 9.2 "Work" circle and potential contributors to fulfillment

per days invested in working, clients that you engage with, and annual income, just to highlight a few.

By identifying these criteria, first, you become decisive towards components that contribute to the whole. Then you can self-assess which parts are fulfilled and which remain unfulfilled. For example, if you spend 12 to 14 hours a day working and your goal is 7 to 9, you may recognize that this component of work is unfulfilled. Working an extra 5 hours a day may be stealing time from other areas of your life that are important to you. You recognize that you need to take action on this, and make some decisions about how to reduce hours at work to reach greater levels of fulfillment in other necessary areas.

When you drill into components that make up the whole, you may find many things you need to balance. *Tweak the dial* is a phrase I use to encourage small, incremental changes toward the goal. Don't try to leap the chasm. Just like New Year's resolutions, leaping head-first is making major changes that may not be feasible to sustain, so the goal is never achieved. Tweaks are incremental changes that build the bridge from where we are to where we want to be and along the way we experience greater levels of wellness without suffering negative emotions like fear, stress, or anxiety, from big changes made hastily.

Another client of mine, Dustin, was working 11 to 13 hours a day, plus weekends and it was burying him. He was missing out on family time and he was experiencing high levels of unfulfillment. Sometimes, for weeks to months at a time, he suffered prolonged periods of depression. As I coached Dustin through identifying his priorities, he was able to drill into his work circle and identify the issues. Long hours, and staff shortages meant not enough delegation and not enough automation. By identifying the barriers, Dustin could implement quick wins that positively impacted the number of hours he was spending at work.

However, these few things did not solve the biggest hurdle. Dustin held himself to a belief system that if he was not at work, watching over things, making things happen, nothing would get done. If he doesn't do it, no one will. If he doesn't respond to a request right away, he will lose customers. Dustin was caught in limiting beliefs of self-importance and fear. When we used reality testing, he admitted that these beliefs, and fears, were absolutely not true. He has a team of highly competent and trusted direct reports, he could delegate; he simply chose not to. He could take his weekends off; he simply chose not to. His customers were loyal, and, in fact, he had a strong referral program.

By tapping into the emotions that were pushing him in the direction of rash decisions (such as long working hours and a lack of delegation and automation), Dustin was able to tweak the dial with solutions that solved the problem and mindset shifts to keep him from making rash decisions.

Consistent self-assessment of fulfillment and the impact of the tweaks surrounding your well-being and success is how you continually move toward balance. This way you can ensure the actions you are taking are helpful and impactful.

When you conduct this exercise, maintaining it as a consistent practice every six to twelve months, the elusive work-life balance will be a thing of the past. You will have taken intentional actions toward the life you want and living the way you want.

Are You Balanced?

Reflection is a gift. Looking back provides opportunities to learn from the past and discover how we want our past experiences to inform our present and future.

Being an entrepreneur is a beautiful thing. As one, I have never had a more fulfilling and meaningful life than the one I lead now. I attribute this to self-actualizing on a regular basis—ensuring my circles are accurate to the life I desire to have. When I wake up each day, I feel this fulfillment more than I intellectualize it. I've only achieved this by looking back and reflecting on what has been meaningful and fulfilling and how I have gone about achieving those things intentionally. It also must include acknowledging when I was off-balance and giving too much of my time, energy, and resources to things that weren't serving me.

I have days where I want to lay in the sun, play in the garden, cancel appointments, and read a book, or take the day off and spend it with my son and husband at the beach. Balanced circles do not protect me from the human experience of sometimes feeling a lack of motivation. It does, however, allow me to quickly notice when I am feeling that way and what to do to reset myself so that I return to balance swiftly.

Sometimes more than an intellectual activity, self-actualization is an emotional one. We feel balanced. Or put another way, harmony. While I've been using the word *balance* frequently throughout this chapter, it may not strike the right chord for you. Balance may be too logical and lacks an extra sense of comfort.

Harmony has a slightly different feel to it, doesn't it? It has a softness. A rhythm. A flow. A sensation.

No matter the word you choose to use, choose wisely. Just as you design the life you wish to have. Be intentional. Be selfish. As mentioned at the beginning of this chapter, to accomplish self-actualization, you need self-leadership. Lead thyself by knowing thyself. This is the essence of being selfish. Not to the detriment of others. To the fulfillment of you.

About Teresa Quinlan

Certified practitioner EQi-2.0 and certified coach CCF, Teresa is the founder of her personal brand, IQ+EQ=TQ, a formula that recognizes the intersection of cognition and emotion. With over thirty years in leadership, and over twenty years in training leaders, she focuses on bringing emotional intelligence into accessible and practical strategies and enables exceptional execution in the most difficult circumstances. Teresa is an executive coach, leadership excellence facilitator, speaker, and consultant. She has co-authored the book, *You Belong Here: HumansFirst Stories*.

Website: www.iqeqtq.com

LinkedIn: www.linkedin.com/in/teresaquinlan12

Whole Person Self-Awareness: The Key to Transformation

Ken Keis

efore acting with purpose and direction, you must understand who you are, what you need to change, and what comes thereafter.

It's nearly impossible to act intentionally when you are unaware of your preferences, gifts, talents, values, beliefs, purpose, and tendencies. If you are unaware, you are living life—day after day, year after year—oblivious to your thoughts and beliefs.

To acknowledge diversity across personalities and provide a framework for self-awareness, development, and understanding of the self and others, CRG Authors and I have collaborated to create the Personality Factors Development Model. I will get into the details of the model in the second half of this chapter, but before that, it's crucial to ground the fundamental importance of self-awareness.

We have met individuals who are utterly unaware of their behavior and conduct. They may even be inappropriate and affect others negatively. They have no clue, often even missing cues.

According to Dr. Tasha Eurich, who wrote the *New York Times* best seller *Insight*, self-awareness is the meta-skill for the twenty-first century and foundational to our success. In her study, 95 percent of individuals believed they were self-aware, and that their opinions self matched what others thought about them. Then, she had her researchers interview those around them and confirm their experiences and opinions. Can you guess what percentage agreed with the self-awareness level of participants? It was an astonishing 10 percent. That means over 85 percent of the population aren't even aware that they don't know.[44]

Self-awareness is even more critical for business owners and entrepreneurs. Without holistic self-awareness and clarity, it's difficult to assess if a business or opportunity is right for you.

Starting Your Own Business Instead of Working as an Employee for Someone Else

A friend called me one day to share a personal dilemma. He had spent the better part of ten years in medical school, to become a doctor. Yet, he disliked his profession. I pried further and asked the obvious, "If you don't like medicine, why are you in this profession?"

He clarified that it had been his parent's dream, "I have invested 20 years of my life in it, what am I to do?". I couldn't help but wonder if he was planning to be miserable for the second half of his life.

During our coaching sessions, I helped my friend thoroughly understand his choices' possible implications. He managed to muster the courage to leave his medical practice and start his own business. He now operates a successful coaching and training company for stressed and burnt-out doctors. He finds this career far more fulfilling.

Is Your Job Making You Miserable?

Many years ago, I had simultaneously become part of no fewer than seven business ventures. The financial success of my training and coaching company seemed to be attracting individuals who wanted me to invest and be a business partner with them. I had to become more self-aware and go through a transition in my entrepreneurial mindset and beliefs.

One of my values is the need for *variety*. At the time, I used that filter, albeit incorrectly, to justify having diverse business interests, including an RV rental business, an alarm and security company, a dairy farm, a car dealership, a mining company, a real estate investment firm, an HIV biotechnology research company, and a training and consulting firm, just to name a few.

I was not even necessarily passionate about some of the businesses, but my friends wanted me to partner with them, and I couldn't say no.

There's nothing wrong with having a couple of (or, in my case, numerous) business interests. However, it was impossible to sustain all those hands-on start-ups and organizations in need of my leadership.

My error was two-fold:

1. I let situational opportunities, what I call 'shiny object disease,' make my decisions. Instead, I should have grounded and centered myself in holistic self-awareness.

2. Instead of saying 'no' to any business ventures, I agreed to participate through the false belief that they contributed to my value of variety.

I realized, via improved self-awareness, that my profession of building a publishing business that included writing, creating online courses, speaking, training, coaching, and consulting provided all the variety I needed.

Your ability to say 'no' is as important as your ability to say 'yes' to your success in life.

Only 13 percent of people worldwide are engaged at work according to a global Gallup survey.[45] You'd imagine that owning your own business would *certainly* change those results. Unfortunately, the statistics for entrepreneurs aren't much better. According to the U.S. Bureau of Labour Statistics, only 50 percent of new businesses survive their first five years, and only one third makes it past year ten.[46]

Why so much failure? Without self-awareness, we choose to engage in opportunities that do not always match our entrepreneurial style, values, and numerous other factors. If your role or business is not a fit, there's no way to sustain the personal energy required to launch or run a venture successfully.

In his book, *Excuses Begone!: How to Change Lifelong, Self-Defeating Thinking Habits*, the late Wayne Dyer put it well: "The reason why awareness of awareness is so powerful is that it immediately puts me in touch with a dimension of myself that knows that: here in awareness, all things are possible." When you become *aware*, you cease being a victim of your circumstances. You own your space.

Are Square Wheels Better than No Wheels at All?

Looking at the following image of the wagon with square wheels[47], what do you see and think?

- What do the square wheels represent as a metaphor for your life—at home and at work? You might answer with words like *struggle*, *difficult*, *inefficient*, *challenge*, *complex*, *toiling*, *stuck*, or even *silly*.

FIGURE 10.1 Working hard when a smarter way is so close, © Performance Management Company

- What about the people pushing the wagon? What do they see? What are their perspectives on this situation?

- Turn to the person pulling the wagon—what is he thinking and experiencing? Is he wondering if anyone will come along to help? Will he look back to see if there is any way to improve the situation?

- What about the round wheels inside the wagon? What do they represent? Do words and ideas like *opportunity, improvement, easier way, upgrade, progress,* or *a different way of doing things* come to mind?

Naturally, this will lead to more questions:

- Why are they stuck—both the leader and the followers?

- Why don't they put the round wheels on the wagon?

- How far away are the round wheels? The wheels appear to be readily available, but the leader and the followers are unaware of the opportunities.

Have you ever met someone dealing with a problem and the answer to their dilemma seems obvious to you? Perhaps the solution is right in front of their eyes, but they still don't get it. They are regrettably completely oblivious to the opportunity.

I admit, in the past, being quick to judge when individuals did not see the obvious course of action. I now understand it was not obvious to them. Rather than standing in judgment, let's shift to helping and coaching people to see the possibilities and positive options.

When we see people deal with their square wheels we can often observe an interesting behavior: Instead of examining the root cause of the problem, they just put more effort into something that is still flawed. Instead of replacing the square wheels with proper round wheels, they would use a tractor to pull the square-wheeled wagon. Instead of working smarter, they work harder.

I see this in individuals, families, teams, organizations, and governments who dedicate themselves to their 'square wheels.' They embrace the certainty of misery rather than the misery of uncertainty. This indicates the blind devotion to broken, unproductive habits, which ultimately causes pain to everyone involved.

Further questions must now be asked:

- Where in your life—personal and interpersonal effectiveness, as well as career fulfillment—are you holding on to square wheels?
- Where have you blindly stayed committed to your square wheels without conscious intention or awareness?

Everyone has a few square wheels, lacking self-awareness or perhaps an outsider's take—including myself. Rather than protecting the status quo, I'm encouraging you to start looking for and using round wheels. As you can see, the round wheels are usually within reach—if you choose to embrace change using new information.

Holistic Self-Awareness: The Key to Success

With the significance of self-awareness established, let's apply this to the Personality Development Factors Model.

Are we a product of nature (born that way) or nurture (input from our environment)? The correct answer is 'yes.' We are a combination of *both* nature and nurture. Each person is born with many parts that form the whole (nature); we gain knowledge and beliefs (nurture) as we live our lives.

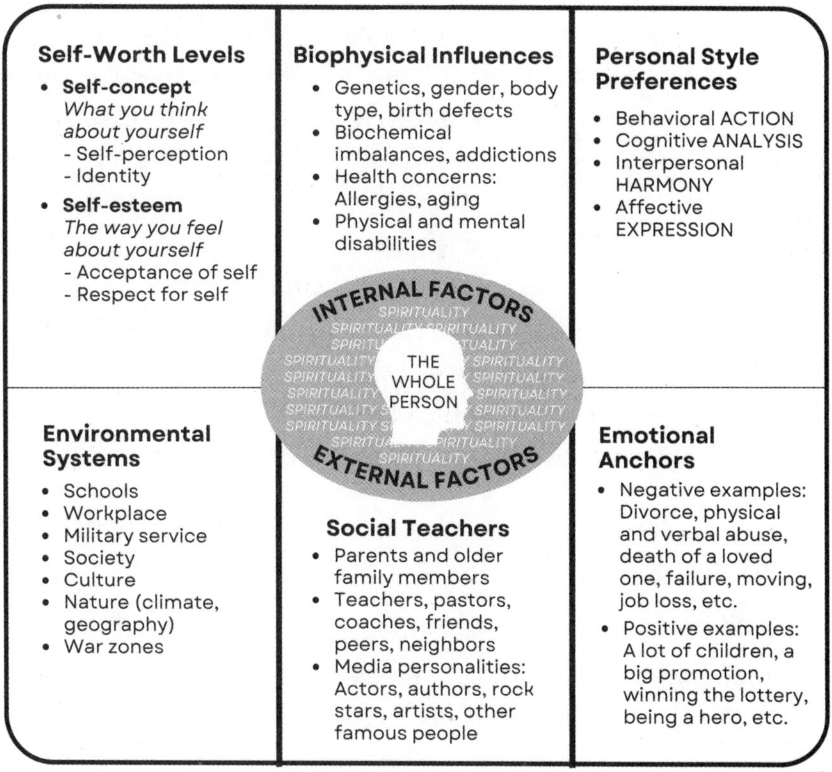

Self-Worth Levels
- **Self-concept**
  What you think about yourself
  - Self-perception
  - Identity
- **Self-esteem**
  The way you feel about yourself
  - Acceptance of self
  - Respect for self

Biophysical Influences
- Genetics, gender, body type, birth defects
- Biochemical imbalances, addictions
- Health concerns: Allergies, aging
- Physical and mental disabilities

Personal Style Preferences
- Behavioral ACTION
- Cognitive ANALYSIS
- Interpersonal HARMONY
- Affective EXPRESSION

INTERNAL FACTORS

THE WHOLE PERSON

SPIRITUALITY

EXTERNAL FACTORS

Environmental Systems
- Schools
- Workplace
- Military service
- Society
- Culture
- Nature (climate, geography)
- War zones

Social Teachers
- Parents and older family members
- Teachers, pastors, coaches, friends, peers, neighbors
- Media personalities: Actors, authors, rock stars, artists, other famous people

Emotional Anchors
- Negative examples: Divorce, physical and verbal abuse, death of a loved one, failure, moving, job loss, etc.
- Positive examples: A lot of children, a big promotion, winning the lottery, being a hero, etc.

FIGURE 10.2 Personality Development Factors Model, © Ken Keis & CRG

Personal Style Preferences

Your personal style is highly related to your entrepreneurial style and strongly affects decision-making and action-taking.[48] Even though you may have learned how to display behavior that is unrelated to your personal style, it always impacts your decision-making; it serves as a filter system through which all your learned behavior must pass.

Your Personal/Entrepreneurial Style is the foundation for your interpersonal style; your preferred business style and the totality of you as a person is called your *personality*.

A study by TalentSmart[49] discovered that less than 30 percent of the population has a solid understanding of their own personal and entrepreneurial preferences. It would follow that about 70 percent of the population has no inkling of how they appear to or interact with others. Individuals are not attuned to their strengths and skills, and without this knowledge, they can't implement them properly. In the study, those oblivious to their personal style had considerably more difficulty handling stress and interpersonal relationships.

The study compared people's levels of self-awareness to their ability to achieve the things they found most important in life:

- Satisfaction with life increases dramatically with self-awareness.

- Self-aware people are far more likely to reach their goals.

- Individuals who are *aware* first take time to learn and then understand their style to better respond to life's challenges and opportunities.

- They can more easily implement the right strategies because they understand their situation and can identify the people who will help them succeed.

- They understand their limitations and adjust their attitude and behavior accordingly to minimize negative impact.

- They know what they want; their awareness motivates them to take the best steps and actions to get where they want to be.

Self-awareness is so imperative to success that it transcends age, intelligence, education, profession, and job level. The TalentSmart study also found that 83 percent of top performers have high self-awareness, no matter their industry or trade. However, just 2 percent of low performers possess the ability to self-inflect.

Individuals who understand their style preferences and tendencies are much more likely to play to their strengths at work and home. Those self-aware individuals also know how to limit the negative impact of their deficiencies and get the desired results.

Style defines people's naturally occurring preferences for engaging with their environment—the unique and consistent ways of reacting to their surroundings. These preferences are usually reflected in their various needs, wants, and values. We know that personal style will remain unchanged throughout a person's lifetime; the style a person has at age two will be evident at age eighty.

Let us be clear, your personal or entrepreneurial style stays consistent; however, the same is not necessarily true for your *personality*. Personality is the totality of who you are. As a result, your personality has both flexibility and stability throughout your life.

To pinpoint the difference between your *personality* and your *personal style*, ask yourself the following:

- Are your job, role, and business a match for your interests, gifts, talents, and personal style?

- Is your personal or entrepreneurial style working *for* you or *against* you?

- What are your personal style patterns and profile and how is it influencing your decisions and choices?

Biophysical Influences: Stress, Health, and Wellness Levels

A topic that begs discussion is mental and emotional health. I suggest we could prevent many mental and emotional health issues. If we check in regularly with ourselves and what might be contributing to our conditions, we can manage mental and emotional health in a more proactive way earlier on. If we check in regularly with ourselves and what might be contributing to our conditions, we can manage mental and emotional health in a more proactive way earlier on.

In 1988, I was moody and had severe emotional swings. One minute I was motivated and excited, next, I just had to go to bed and sleep. My doctor said I was manic-depressive and put me on antidepressants. About a week into treatment, I was ready to crawl right out of my skin—I was irritable and not feeling better, let alone well at all.

A friend said, "Ken, you don't have a depression problem. It sounds more like a biophysical condition." At my insistence, the doctor then conducted a glucose tolerance test (GTT). After giving you pure sugar to drink, they draw blood every thirty minutes for six hours, to measure glucose levels in your bloodstream.

The test revealed I had extreme hypoglycemia, a blood sugar condition. When I consume sugar, my pancreas does not produce insulin in the correct proportion, which causes all kinds of complications. My personality changed significantly because of the wild swings in my blood sugar levels. It was a biochemical state. It had nothing to do with depression.

Here is the teaching point: no matter how motivated or enjoyable your work or business might be, if you are stressed or unwell, you will never be able to sustain engagement or productivity levels. According to the World Health Organization (WHO), up to 85 percent of the global population lead lifestyles that increase the risk of illnesses and stress. Adjusting our lifestyles can reduce these risks.

Do you know your wellness and stress levels and what is contributing to your condition?

For many the question is too big, so we need to break it down—so we can get to the potential root cause(s). Areas to consider for wellness self-awareness:

1. Distress—Physically, Physiologically, Behavioral Symptoms: Your condition leaves clues to how well or stressed you are. From headaches to insomnia, these symptoms are indications

of your stress levels. Are you paying attention or ignoring the signs?

2. Interpersonal Stress Levels: What would others say about the health of your relationships, both personally and professionally? Tension produces cortisol, a hormone that regulates your immunity and stress levels. This occurs when withdrawing from conflict—avoiding and stuffing—to aggressive outbursts, neither of which are healthy.

3. Wellness: Nutritional and Lifestyle Stress: You're likely familiar with the expression *you are what you eat*. Unhealthy diets will lower your energy, and depending on the severity, can lead to chronic illness. Lifestyle refers to fitness and recreational activities, which includes spending time with friends, physical activity, and engaging in your community. A recent study confirmed that the top two factors contributing to our longevity are levels of generosity and having loving relationships.

4. Time Stress: There is no such thing as time management; rather, it is how you manage your activities and prioritize your time. If you are constantly living your life without margins and working 80–100 hours a week—the likelihood is that you are stressed.

5. Occupational Stress: The number one factor contributing to stress globally is a person's work or business. Ask yourself this question: Do you own the business or does the business own you? Don't stay in a business or job that is making you miserable. You could be in the perfect role or business but have a toxic environment or partners—make sure you pay attention to these factors.

This list is just a cursory check-in with your self-awareness, stress, and wellness levels. A deep dive will allow you to assess yourself internally and become self-aware.

Research also links our cognitive abilities to wellness and weight. People must change their biophysical condition before they can implement other desired changes.

Are any stressors hindering your ability to engage in life the way you want? If your answer is 'yes,' what are those influences costing you in terms of your lifestyle or quality of life? You need to be willing to do something about it.

Self-Worth Levels

You and I may have a similar personal style. However, if one of us has high self-worth and the other has low self-worth, we could respond differently to similar events. Self-worth is the part of your personality that determines personal value and importance. It is the area of our thinking that evaluates our behavior, appearance, feelings, thoughts, and abilities. It outlines both the level of appreciation we have for ourselves and the way we feel about our inherent worth—what we believe we need to be or do to have value as a person.

Self-worth is a basic human need, essential to normal, healthy development. High self-worth helps provide flexibility, strength, and a capacity to regenerate. It relates to increased levels of mental health, life success, and happiness.

Research has shown that individuals with lower self-esteem have a lesser ability to contribute to society than people with higher self-worth. Low self-worth undermines all areas of human interaction and diminishes resilience in the face of life's problems. Low self-worth can stunt psychological and emotional growth. Overwhelmingly, the majority of research supports the opinion that overall, there are strong benefits to having high self-worth.

Self-worth is not only a source of motivation and energy to engage in life, it consists of psychological vulnerability, otherwise known as resilience. Dr. Nathaniel Branden, author of

Our Urgent Need for Self-Esteem, sums up our thoughts regarding the importance of self-worth.

According to Dr. Branden, self-worth provides the confidence of coping with life's basic challenges and being worthy of happiness. It consists of two components:

1. Self-Efficacy: Confidence in our ability to think, learn, choose, and make appropriate decisions

2. Self-Respect: Confidence in our right to be happy and the belief that achievement, success, friendship, respect, love, and fulfillment are appropriate to us

Our self-worth can vary depending on the situation. When I was in high school, my self-worth was low, yet at that same time, I was succeeding in my agricultural youth movement. I was a national award winner and one of only five chosen from the entire country for a trip to Europe. What I started to notice— through self-awareness—was that in family situations, my perception of self was different than in other situations. We can think and feel differently about ourselves in distinctive situations. The important point to remember is that our self-worth levels are learned, and whatever has been learned can also be unlearned.

Environmental Systems

Culture and environment may include any experiential stimulus we receive from our surroundings—an external experience. That includes all the general influences we are exposed to as a result of being members of various social, cultural, and ethnic groups.

Environmental stimulus excludes the influence of people who have functioned, in some way, as significant role models. For instance, while a person's whole family unit would have a cultural and environmental impact on us, the role played by a specific relative of an individual would belong in the Social-Teacher category.

The environmental systems that surround us as we grow up strongly influence us. The first such system is our family of origin—the family unit we grow up with from birth to young adulthood.

Looking into the Environmental-Systems category, personality is affected by exposure to and observations of family interactions and surroundings. Other environmental systems include schools you have attended, towns or cities where you lived, the countryside where you grew up, the society and cultures, military service, and associations and organizations to which you belong.

In our research conducted with 4,000 successful entrepreneurs, many of the 28 success factors we identified had to do with their background and previous exposure to environmental systems. This usually influenced their mindset around their business. For example, one factor confirmed that growing up to help run a family business was an indication that they would be open to starting and running their own business.

Social Teachers & Values

What would it mean if you could make the right decision every time? It is not a play on words, but a powerful and practical approach to living your life. Today, we have more choices and options than at any other point in the history of humankind, so it can be challenging to filter through and decide effectively. Everyone has internal values that are fulfilling, inspiring, and motivating when present.

In our work and research, we discuss two types of values. Behavioral values are internal motivators, with each contributing to your fulfillment and enjoyment in life. These motivators can be further broken down to include challenges, expertise, or independence.

If someone stopped you on the street and asked you to rank your top five to seven values in their order of priority, as well as how your life represents these values, could you do it? My experience after conducting hundreds of workshops using our values assessment is that most cannot pinpoint them confidently. Yet, several research papers show that those who are clear about their values are less stressed, more resilient, better decision-makers, and more objective in their communications and conversations.

Some values are more contextual, like family or wellness. Both types of values are important to clarify, confirm, and actuate. Contextual values are shaped and formed via the input we have experienced or allowed into our lives, including the family of origin. Custom practices and behaviors highly influence what you will find most valuable. I grew up on a dairy farm and was taught the significance of physical labor. Taking time off was a treat. My parents constantly reminded me that they worked fourteen years without a single day off. When I went back to the farm after college and wanted to have a couple of weekends to myself each month, they quickly adjusted my work schedule to two half-days off.

As one of my early employers, my parents taught me that hard work comes first and that there is little time for play. I have put 100 percent effort into every position I have held since, no matter the working conditions or salary. The work ethic was instilled into my mind long ago as an important value.

We observe and look up to others as role models, and develop an understanding of which behaviors are desirable and which should be avoided. Frequently, the learning occurs indirectly and often without our being aware. We learn how to behave from watching and imitating other people's behavior.

The American Academy of Pediatrics confirmed that a child's input reflects their output. Social teachers can be video games, social media, music, and the like. Exposure to media violence through television, movies, music, and video games can contribute to various physical and mental health problems for children and adolescents, including desensitization to violence and aggressive behavior, nightmares, fear, and depression.

The Social-Teacher category includes people who have raised us from birth. Specifically, we learn from family members we frequently meet, especially those older than us. All our peers growing up, and other significant individuals such as teachers, pastors, and athletic coaches would have potentially impacted us with their values. Even media personalities, historical figures, authors, sports celebrities, and movie stars might be part of the influences in this category. They likely would have had a significant impact on our thinking and behavior. Your values are shaped and influenced by the input you are allowing into your space and mind.

It's time to be brutally honest with yourself. Observing who you are allowing as input or social teachers for yourself and your family can be highly indicative of what influences your values.

- What kind of books or magazines did you buy—if any—last month? Are they positive and educational, or frivolous?

- If I looked at your home library, what would I find?

- What about other media—television, music, movies, social media? What was the content? How much time did you spend using each of those media sources?

Emotional Anchors

This category consists of any experience that has caused us a strong emotional recall or response—positive or negative. After a major event shocks or affects our systems, we are never the same again. The memory of it penetrates beyond our reasoning into our subconscious and leaves us changed (with a positive or negative trigger) from who we were before the event happened.

Growing up on the dairy farm, we were always conscious of safety around farm equipment. My father was harvesting silage and cutting grass for winter storage. One day after school, I hitched a ride in one of the silage wagons with chains and sharp spikes for unloading the silage at the storage location. The driver pulled the silage wagon up to a powerful blower that threw silage six stories high. In the process, he had forgotten I was in the silage wagon. He had powered up the belt that fed the blower and was about to turn on the silage wagon. I knew I had to get out of the wagon, or I would be injured or killed.

As I jumped out, I slipped onto the conveyor belt that fed into the blower. I was seconds away from death when a hired hand pulled me off the belt. I never rode inside another silage wagon again.

That experience is an emotional anchor for me. It has made me extremely safety conscious around any type of machinery or equipment. My three favorite words are safety, safety, and safety.

An emotional anchor is any event or memory that prompts a strong emotional response. As a teen, I was very involved in the rural youth program called 4-H Canada. This program offered leadership development and travel opportunities. At age 16, I earned a trip to Toronto's national conference and was selected to speak to over 400 delegates and sponsors. I vividly recall the nerves and the excitement I felt! After that experience, I knew I wanted to be a speaker and a communicator to large groups. That is a strong and positive emotional anchor for me.

The main point is that after an intense emotional experience, our personalities and behavior can change; we do not remain the same.

Are you aware of how you have been affected by your experiences?

Examples of emotional anchors:

Negative possibilities: Divorce, physical abuse, death of a loved one, failure, moving, job loss, natural catastrophes

Positive possibilities: Raising children, a promotion for your dream job, winning the lottery, becoming a heroEveryone will respond uniquely to events. Some will be traumatized; others will not. What emotional anchors are supporting or hindering you?

Beliefs and Spirituality

At the center of the Personality Development Factors Model, you will notice a person's facial profile. Next to the profile, the word *spirituality* is written many times. Spirituality is part of our model because a person's beliefs and spiritual perspective influence behavior, choices, values, and life satisfaction.

In our model, we are not referring to humanistic, watered-down versions of spirituality, typically unspecific beliefs. We are referring to the foundational beliefs on which our lives exist and function. That is the deepest level of awareness we can seek to achieve.

For many, true fulfillment is achieved through understanding their relationship with spirituality. Confirming and determining your self-awareness includes going on a personal quest to find the level of significance that spirituality plays in your life. If you're a spiritual person, or if not, take some time to reflect on the following questions:

- Are human beings spiritual? How can we know?

- If we are spiritual, what does that mean? What is the truth on the subject?

- How can I tell spiritual truth from falsehood?
- Does God exist? Who or what does God represent?

Our lives operate under natural laws and truths. Regardless of our opinions, the rules do not change. One example is gravity. It exists even if we don't understand or accept it. When people believed that the world was flat, their collective opinion did not make it so. The principle of natural law applies equally to spirituality. Our focus should be on discovering spiritual truth, not on creating it because no one can create spiritual truth—just as no one can create gravity.

We include spirituality as part of our Personality Development Factors Model because beliefs highly influence choices and success in life. Even if you say you believe in nothing—believing in *nothing* is just as much a spiritual factor, as this will influence what you do or don't do in life.

If you are going to understand yourself and others, the core of your spirituality matters—and matters deeply—to your inner peace, fulfillment, and your ability to positively impact others.

I've provided you with a starting framework for holistic self-awareness; however, it's important to note that this is the beginning, not the end! The next step after self-awareness is self-management, where you are in charge of self and aware of the impact that these factors are having on you and on others to select behaviors and choices that are positive and fulfilling.

The final step is self-mastery. At this point, you will have developed your self-awareness and deliberately conduct yourself in a way and direction that you desire mostly unconsciously. Now take a moment and confirm what round wheels you are able and willing to install onto your wagon of life.

About Ken Keis

Ken is an expert on leadership, purpose, and personality and behavioral assessments. He is the CEO & President of Consulting Resource Group International Inc., which provides learning resources to individuals and development professionals across the globe. He is an internationally known speaker and consultant. Ken is the author of *Why Aren't You More Like Me?*, *Deliberate Leadership*, and *The Quest For Purpose*, and 500+ articles. Best-selling authors Kenneth Blanchard, Jim Kouzes, and Marshall Goldsmith have all endorsed Ken's work.

Website: www.kenkeis.com

LinkedIn: www.linkedin.com/in/kenkeiscrgleader

Four Powerful Mindset Shifts to Help You Conquer Love, Overcome Death, and Succeed in Business

Alex Brueckmann

I'm sitting on the balcony of our apartment in New Westminster. I'm thinking about how lucky I am to be holding my baby boy, and I can't stop a few tears from rolling down my cheeks as I think about my late father. I honestly don't know whether these are tears of joy or tears of grief. Maybe it's a bit of both mixed together. I can't believe I've survived the past three months without a total mental breakdown. Looking back now, with some clarity, at that moment, I couldn't understand how I got past the feeling of constantly being overwhelmed.

A few months prior, I was founding a new business while my girlfriend was experiencing a very challenging last trimester of her pregnancy. I was worried and anxious for her. At the same time, my father was suffering from terminal cancer. I wasn't sure I could keep it all together. I felt the duty to provide for my family even as these other areas of my life unraveled.

My emotions were constantly changing, like being on a rollercoaster ride. I wanted to be there for my girlfriend, dad and mom, and clients—all at the same time. I felt like I was in a dark tunnel, and I needed to push through these challenging months hoping that things would get better and easier to manage.

As things unfolded, I'm sure you can imagine, that's not exactly what happened. Things spiraled quite dramatically. Quickly, my dad passed away, and my son was born two weeks later. I had no idea how to cope with all these extreme emotions at the same time.

I was experiencing both crushing sadness and grief at the loss of my father and the overwhelming joy of becoming a first-time dad. And eight weeks later, we would pack up our lives, and move from Germany to Canada at the beginning of a global pandemic. Sitting on my balcony, in April 2020, I had to take a moment to try and catch my breath.

When faced with difficult business challenges, crushing loss from death, or overwhelming emotions from love, it's easy to see only chaos and it can be a struggle to keep your emotions under control. I will share four powerful mindsets that helped me conquer love, overcome death, and succeed in business. This way you can further explore how simple changes can impact your life and your business. By shifting your mindset, you will discover how to unleash your innovative and creative brain to build a life you can be proud of, and lead with an amazing living legacy.

Mindset Beats Skillset

It might be shocking that the right mindset can be more relevant than skill when approaching long-term success—skill matters, but only so much. Over the long run, people with the right attitude can outperform those who started with better skills. Adjusting your mindset allows you to focus on thinking smarter, with more nuance, and with more ingenuity, and find multiple paths to success.

It is true in sports when people who've flown under the radar suddenly win championships and trophies. Every overnight success has been years in the making; success cannot be credited to beginner's luck. We've also seen it in the entertainment world where great artists die unknown and others, with questionable talent, win Grammys or Oscars.

In business, mindset beats skill every time. If we have the skill but lack the mindset, the chance is that we lack the momentum to turn our dreams into reality.

But what exactly is *mindset*? Mindset is more than believing in yourself. It is more than giving yourself a pep talk in front of the mirror before an important meeting. Rather than talking about mindset in general, I want to give you something concrete and actionable. Let's explore four specific mindset shifts that will help you shift and succeed.

Drop the 'F' from Fomo

First, let's talk about the fear of missing out, otherwise known as FOMO. It happens when everyone in our circle of friends has tickets to this hot new artist's show—and you feel like the only one who has never heard of them. Then we buy tickets as well, just in case. We do it because everyone else is doing it, and we don't want to miss out on something everyone else is raving about.

Feeling anxious or scared of missing out is natural. But it drives us into pursuing actions that are falsely presented as opportunities. FOMO occurs because we don't have clear priorities or strategies to reach the desired end goal. It happens to people who succeed by winging it or by hoping for the best. It's a fluke. If they are successful, it's sheer luck. This type of success is accidental rather than intentionally created. It's rarely repeatable, nor scalable.

If we let fear drive our business decisions, we are busy wasting our most valuable asset—our attention—on stuff that doesn't matter. As a result, we actually do miss out on what matters. On an individual level, that might lead to poor job performance, a lack of career advancement, or even job loss. On a corporate level, FOMO can be detrimental. It leads to 'copy-cat' strategies, with companies copying whatever the competition does first. We all know clarity, direction, and differentiation are keys to success, not copying others.

The first mindset change can occur when shifting from *FOMO* to *JOMO*—otherwise known as the *joy* of missing out. The good news is that we can make this shift in no time. All we have to do is define our priorities in life and business.

Write them down. Writing crystallizes our thinking. The process helps us understand what matters to us and how we will achieve our goals. By writing them down, we see whether our ideas and goals are attainable. This piece of collateral that we create by writing down priorities and goals becomes our go-to resource for decision-making. It gives us clarity and direction. When an opportunity comes our way, we benchmark it against that collateral. Ask yourself a few questions factual mistake:

- How does it help me reach my goals faster?
- Where does it fit into my priorities?
- Can I afford to focus my attention on this now?

Asking these questions will help you tell a shiny object from a real opportunity. Instead of falling into the FOMO trap, we can put ourselves in a position to evaluate any situation. For example, a great idea. It might be a good opportunity later, however, it doesn't help me reach my immediate goals. This evaluation indicates that I should pass.

Inevitably, it would be best if you let it go. For any business owner, knowing what not to focus on, or rather what to avoid, is just as important as knowing what we want. Knowing what not to do is extremely liberating. It sets us free from the urge to follow expectations or strategies, potentially losing ourselves along the way. Instead, we create our own path, our own success story. Don't do things just because they worked for someone else. Don't waste time copying others in your personal life or business—be an original.

Aim for Speed And Agility

The second mindset shift we will talk about is from perfectionism to speed. My job involves helping businesses create roadmaps to build the future they envision. In other words, I'm a strategy facilitator. When clients ask, "Alex, how long does it take to design a perfect business strategy?" I shrug my shoulders, as I never did. This answer is not what they expect to hear—but it's the truth.

As previously stated, I create a sense of JOMO by writing down goals and priorities, which is another way of saying, "write down your strategy." But please: don't try to design a perfect strategy. There is no such thing as a perfect strategy. You can tweak a strategy forever, seemingly improving it further and further. But you're not necessarily making it perfect. What you are actually doing is standing in the way of implementation, learning along the way, and succeeding over time. This makes perfectionism the enemy of growth and progress.

We can overcome a perfectionist mindset and embrace an attitude of speed and agility. A speed mindset gives us the momentum to get us going, whereas agility helps us avoid getting stuck. Combined, the two help us streamline progress. Aligning a business around an 80 percent strategy—leaving 20 percent for uncertainty—gives us enough clarity and direction to get going. Implementing a strategy with speed and agility will yield more significant results than spending months refining a strategy to the illusion of perfection, all while standing still and wasting time. Aim to start fast and remain agile to course-correct along the way.

I believe that life and business are not about being perfect, being right, or being wrong. It is about striving for excellence. Learning, sometimes through mistakes, occurs by improving and adjusting our approaches one step at a time, while having our vision front and center. When designing our priorities, clarity, and direction, we want to look out for *good enough*, not for perfect. Stop planning and start moving when you feel your strategy is ready to test.

Managing speed and agility is also essential in our personal lives. We may have a perfect plan in place. And then something messes up that plan. In March 2020, my family was six weeks away from moving from Germany to Canada. Then the first wave of COVID-19 was exploding, and German authorities locked down the country. Our seemingly perfect plan went down the drain at that point, and we needed to act swiftly and decisively. I knew we had to get on one of the few remaining flights, or we would potentially miss our assigned window to immigrate to Canada. Instead of a plan, we now had chaos.

Try to put yourselves into that situation: imagine you have to re-plan a move to another continent within nine days, under newly imposed lockdown conditions, with a newborn in your arms, while mourning the loss of a loved one, anxious about COVID-19. What do you do? How do you prioritize?

Emotionally, this was an extreme time for us, and we asked ourselves what it would take to make things happen, even against all odds. So, we allowed ourselves to be emotionally agile. Even if the world around us was on fire, we embraced the beauty of the intimate moments of love with our baby. While everything around us was overwhelming, from the death of my dad and the fear involved at the start of the pandemic, being emotionally agile allowed us to stay mentally sane.

Agility gave us the strength we needed to function and make the sheer impossible happen. We packed our lives into seven suitcases, made it safe and sound to Vancouver, and we've been building our lives in Canada since. We chose speed and agility over perfectionism while learning and adjusting along the way.

Embrace Abundance

Some might correlate the term abundance to the subject of pop-spirituality or pseudoscience, like manifesting. That is not the same meaning as abundance in mindset. We can gain a better understanding of the abundance mindset by comparing it to a less ideal scarcity mindset.

Let's dissect the two: if you see someone else thriving, you may feel there is not enough room for you, you begin to panic, and you are in a scarcity mindset. Like the colleague who just got a raise or a promotion, you begin to feel that there may not be enough space for your own raise or career advancement. Or if someone in the buffet line in front of you takes the last slices of that pizza that you have been craving. You fear there won't be any pizza left when it's your turn. That's your scarcity mindset kicking in, blinding you from the fact that they will eventually replenish the pizza as a regular occurrence.

A scarcity mindset pits us against each other; if you win, then I will lose. Our competitiveness is forced into overdrive, like fight or flight. We feel there are never enough resources. The scarcity mindset tells us that everything is limited, like career shifts we can make, business opportunities we can pursue, and our potential to learn or to find love in life. Overthinking in a scarcity mindset is unnecessary because if we open our hearts and minds, we see that most of the time, there is more than enough.

This realization comes with shifting from a scarcity to an abundance mindset. It means understanding situations as full instead of empty; there are more than enough resources available, recognizing new possibilities internally and externally. Abundance opens our minds to options that otherwise would have been invisible to us.

In business, an abundance mindset is crucial for creating a winning strategy. It's about exploring possibilities, curiosity, and daring to dream. It's about creating hope. Allowing ourselves to be in an abundance mindset will bring about new perspectives, thoughts, and discussions that were previously unclear to us because we listen deeply and build on each other's creativity. A scarcity mindset shuts others and their ideas down. We say 'yes, but. . .' rather than 'yes, and. . . .' Remember, while JOMO helps you prioritize by saying 'no' to many unnecessary things, an abundance mindset keeps you open-minded so that you don't say 'no' pre-maturely. Allow yourself to be abundant first to evaluate and make informed decisions.

Abundance also helped me overcome the loss of my father. Emotionally, this was undoubtedly the biggest challenge for me to overcome. While I traditionally dealt with my emotions by myself, I felt I probably needed to seek out additional resources this time. The emotional rollercoaster I had been riding was controlling my mood swings. I was starting to fight with my girlfriend over petty things instead of relying on her for emotional support. This time, I didn't want to mess up and told myself there must be someone out there—outside of my circle of friends and family—who can help me. This might sound obvious, but my next move was a sign that I was starting to embrace an abundance mindset. While it felt weird at first, I reached out to a psychologist. As an additional resource in my life, she helped me overcome the loss of my dad.

Grow Beyond a Fixed Mind

There's one last mindset shift to cover, and I'm sure you are familiar with the term 'growth mindset.' But what does it mean? A growth mindset is the opposite of a fixed mindset. Instead of thinking in limited realities and absolutes, we search for options, opportunities, and alternatives, based on a desire to learn. So the fourth mindset shift is from a fixed mindset to a growth mindset.

A growth mindset helps us see our faults or mistakes as learning opportunities. A fixed mindset would make us think 'I failed' or 'I'll never make it.' A growth mindset allows us to find new ways of doing things, enabling us to try something different instead of giving up before crossing the finish line.

When I was younger, I had a reasonably fixed mindset. And there was so much that my fixed mind couldn't make sense of until I realized I could do something about it. I became an avid reader, curious about so many things. I started to embrace learning as a path to overcome my fixed mindset.

Rather than talking in statements, trying to make things fit into what we already know, we should ask questions like: 'what am I missing?' or 'how could I use this negative experience and turn it into something positive?'

When we are in a growth mindset, we realize that nothing is ever *too hard*. Stagnant terms like this come from a fixed mindset. If we allow ourselves to add some perspective and the time factor, we realize, although we don't know how something works *yet*, we'll figure it out eventually.

How to Enact the Mindset Shifts

So how can we make these mindset shifts happen in our lives? And where would they be helpful for us right now? Adam Grant, one of the world's leading organizational psychologists, describes two concepts that help us: challenge networks and confident humility.[50]

A challenge network is a team around us that consists of people who can disagree, agreeably, and give brutally honest feedback without being personal or aggressive. The purpose of a challenge network is to help question assumptions, overcome blind spots, and counterbalance potential weaknesses in our thinking. A challenge network makes us see flaws—and plays the devil's advocate—in our plans. You'll tackle the speed, in execution and learning, by building a reliable challenge network.

Moreover, according to Grant, confident humility is "having faith in our capability while appreciating that we may not have the right solution or even be addressing the right problem. That gives us enough doubt to reexamine our old knowledge and enough confidence to pursue new insights." The sweet spot of confidence is when we believe in ourselves and simultaneously doubt that we have all the right tools in place.

Opening this chapter, I shared a memory of sitting on the balcony with my newborn baby at the beginning of the pandemic. A few weeks ago, a friend reminded me of that time, and expressed that she had been concerned. She thought I would break down under all those emotions and stressors. She asked me how I got through this time without completely losing it.

I didn't have an immediate answer but did a bit of digging. And I saw that those four mindset shifts—JOMO, speed and agility, abundance, and growth—helped me get through this most challenging time of my life.

What if I hadn't embraced these four mindsets? My life would be so much different.

Learning to no longer fear missing out on opportunities and shifting to JOMO helped me avoid distractions in business. I focused on what mattered and, as a result, had enough quality time that I could spend with my family. Seeing my son grow up and having an active role in his life is the most fulfilling part of my life. Being with him as much as possible is a direct result of not letting shiny objects water down my focus, no longer wasting time, and learning to prioritize.

If I didn't embrace the joy of missing out, I would have spent a lot more time worrying about the needs of my business while investing unnecessary time and energy. It would have taken so much more away from the special moments.

In collaboration with this, abundance made me see options that otherwise would have been invisible to me, especially in the context of leaning into a new culture, in a new country, and overcoming the loss of my father. If I hadn't embraced an abundance mindset, I wouldn't have had the courage and determination to start a business and make it a successful one. Scarcity thinking would have held me back from taking the risks involved.

A growth mindset helps me rise to the challenge and grow into the role of being a first-time dad in my mid-40s and loving it with every fiber of my being.

Speed and agility helped me avoid overthinking and getting stuck. Without having such a flexible mindset, I wouldn't have gotten the plane tickets to Canada. We would have missed our window of opportunity and lost our residency. If I hadn't moved to Canada, I wouldn't have met the people I work with today.

Without these mindset shifts, I would still be the same person with the same skills. But creating winning strategies in business and our personal lives is about turning hopes and dreams into reality. Winning strategies require a growth mindset as much as an abundance of thinking, speed, and the guts to go for JOMO. Mindset trumps skill.

About Alex Brueckmann

Alex is a strategy practitioner and keynote speaker who helps businesses create clarity and strategic direction. Having worked with entrepreneurs, business owners, and corporate leaders for two decades, he is a trusted advisor to businesses large and small.

Alex is the author of *The Strategy Legacy* (2023); the book introduces the business strategy and leadership framework of the Nine Elements of Organizational Identity. Corresponding resources are available on his website, such as free toolkits and online courses.

Website: www.brueckmann.ca

LinkedIn: www.linkedin.com/in/alexanderbrueckmann

Notes

1. Schurenberg, Eric. "In the End, You Have to Say, Screw It. Just Do It." Inc.com. Inc., February 21, 2013. https://www.inc.com/eric-schurenberg/sir-richard-branson-in-the-end-you-have-to-say-screw-it-just-do-it.html.
2. Gans, Joshua, Erin Scott, and Scott Stern. "Strategy for Start-Ups." *Harvard Business Review*, May 2018, 44–51.
3. "An Overview of Porsche - Strategy, Data, Facts and Locations - Porsche AG." Porsche AG - Dr. Ing. h.c. F. Porsche AG, 2021. https://www.porsche.com/international/aboutporsche/overview/strategy2025/.
4. "Our Values." Boeing, June 17, 2020. https://www.boeing.com/principles/values.page.
5. Isidore, Chris. "Boeing's 737 Max Debacle Could Be the Most Expensive Corporate Blunder Ever." CNN, November 17, 2020. https://www.cnn.com/2020/11/17/business/boeing-737-max-grounding-cost/index.html.
6. Porter, Michael E. *Competitive Strategy*. New York: Free, 2004.
7. Cowley, Stacy, and Emily Flitter. "Wells Fargo's Ex-Chief Fined $17.5 Million over Fake Accounts." *New York Times*, January 23, 2020. https://www.nytimes.com/2020/01/23/business/wells-fargo-ceo-fine.html#:~:text=But%20on%20Thursday%2C%20Wells%20Fargo's,accounts%20on%20millions%20of%20customers.
8. Senge, Peter M. *The Fifth Discipline: The Art and Practice of the Learning Organization*. New York: Doubleday, 1994.
9. "Data and Analytics." BCG. https://www.bcg.com/en-ca/capabilities/digital-technology-data/data-analytics.
10. Malnight, Thomas, Charles Dhanaraj, and Ivy Buche. "Put Purpose at the Core of Your Strategy." *Harvard Business Review*, August 27, 2019. https://hbr.org/2019/09/put-purpose-at-the-core-of-your-strategy.
11. Schaninger, Bill, Bruce Simpson, Han Zhang, and Chris Zhu. "Demonstrating Corporate Purpose in the Time of Coronavirus." McKinsey & Company. McKinsey & Company, March 13, 2021.

https://www.mckinsey.com/business-functions/people-and-organizational-performance/our-insights/demonstrating-corporate-purpose-in-the-time-of-coronavirus.

12. Dhingra, Naina, and Bill Schaninger. "The Search for Purpose at Work." McKinsey & Company, January 19, 2022. https://www.mckinsey.com/business-functions/people-and-organizational-performance/our-insights/the-search-for-purpose-at-work.

13. Jardine, Alexandra. "As Parties Resume, Heineken Says Don't Mix up Your Beer Bottles." Ad Age, July 14, 2021. https://adage.com/creativity/work/heineken-home-gatherings/2338136#:~:text=The%20latest%20global%20spot%20from,green%20bottles%20of%20Heineken's%20brew.

14. "Single Use Ain't Sexy." Good Design, October 13, 2021. https://good-design.org/projects/single-use-aint-sexy/.

15. "Carib Glassworks Ltd." Carib Glass, Recycle. https://caribglass.com/recycle.

16. "Briefing: What Are Scope 3 Emissions?" *The Carbon Trust*, 2022. https://www.carbontrust.com/resources/briefing-what-are-scope-3-emissions.

17. "Coffee Recycling, Bio-Bean–Recycling Spent Coffee Grounds." bio-bean renewals, January 10, 2022. https://www.bio-bean.com/renewals/coffee-recycling.

18. "Sustainable Consumption and Production." United Nations. https://www.un.org/sustainabledevelopment/sustainable-consumption-production/.

19. Helena Helmersson and Jesper Brodin: Talking Sustainability. YouTube, 2021. https://www.youtube.com/watch?v=iW0KW5I_q4k.

20. "Ethical and Responsible Business Practices." Nestlé Global. https://www.nestle.com/sustainability/responsible-business.

21. Airbnb Co-Founder Joe Gebbia on Leading with Intention. YouTube, 2022. https://www.youtube.com/watch?v=fPRiSlePIj4.

22. "About." Airbnb.org. Accessed July 25, 2022. https://www.airbnb.org/about#:~:text=Airbnb.org%20%2D%20About,through%20the%20Open%20Homes%20initiative.

23. Bloom, Nicholas, James Liang, John Roberts, and Zhichun Jenny Ying. "Does Working from Home Work? Evidence from a Chinese Experiment." *Stanford University Quarterly Journal of Economics*, 2013. https://doi.org/10.3386/w18871.

24. Hill, Napoleon. *Think and Grow Rich*. Quebec: TGR, 2022.

25. "Organizational Culture: Managing Your Culture by Design Rather than Default." Steelcase, March 4, 2022. https://www.steelcase.com/research/articles/topics/culture/organizational-culture-managing-culture-design-rather-default/.

26. Schaninger, Bill, Alexander DiLeonardo, Taylor Lauricella, and Stephanie Smallets. "How Organizations Can Build Healthy Employee Habits." McKinsey & Company, July 6, 2020. https://www.mckinsey.com/business-functions/people-and-organizational-performance/our-insights/the-organization-blog/how-organizations-can-build-healthy-employee-habits.
27. Dreyer, Chris. "Remote Vs. In-Person Work: Pros And Cons To Weigh As A Business Owner." *Forbes Magazine*, April 21, 2022. https://www.forbes.com/sites/forbesagencycouncil/2021/11/08/remote-vs-in-person-work-pros-and-cons-to-weigh-as-a-business-owner/?sh=3a4b02937cf9.
28. Baker, Mary, and Teresa Zuech. "Gartner Survey Finds 90% of HR Leaders Will Allow Employees to Work Remotely Even after COVID-19 Vaccine Is Available." Gartner, December 15, 2020. https://www.gartner.com/en/newsroom/press-releases/12-14-2020-gartner-survey-finds-ninety-percent-of-hr-leaders-will-allow-employees-to-work-remotely-even-after-covid-19-vaccine-is-available.
29. Sull, Charles, Donald Sull, and Ben Zweig. "Toxic Culture Is Driving the Great Resignation." *MIT Sloan Management Review*, January 11, 2022. https://sloanreview.mit.edu/article/toxic-culture-is-driving-the-great-resignation.
30. Neal, Stephanie, Jazmine Boatman, and Bruce Watt. "Global Leadership Forecast." DDI, 2021. https://www.ddiworld.com/glf.
31. "A Call for Accountability and Action - Deloitte." Deloitte Touche Tohmatsu Limited. Accessed August 3, 2022. https://www2.deloitte.com/content/dam/Deloitte/global/Documents/2021-deloitte-global-millennial-survey-report.pdf.
32. Dhingra, Naina, and Bill Schaninger. "The Search for Purpose at Work." McKinsey & Company, January 19, 2022. https://www.mckinsey.com/business-functions/people-and-organizational-performance/our-insights/the-search-for-purpose-at-work.
33. Collins, Jim. *Good to Great: Why Some Companies Make the Leap. . . and Others Don't*. London: Random House, 2001.
34. Sorenson, Susan. "How Employees' Strengths Make Your Company Stronger." Gallup, May 9, 2022. https://news.gallup.com/businessjournal/167462/employees-strengths-company-stronger.aspx.
35. Lencioni, Patrick. *The Five Dysfunctions of a Team: Team Assessment*. San Francisco, CA: Pfeiffer, 2012.
36. Overton, Amy, and Ann Lowry. "Conflict Management: Difficult Conversations with Difficult People." *Clinics in Colon and Rectal Surgery* 26, no. 04 (2013): 259–64. https://doi.org/10.1055/s-0033-1356728.

37. Gandhi, Vipula, and Jennifer Robison. "The 'Great Resignation' Is Really the 'Great Discontent'." Gallup, May 19, 2022. https://www.gallup.com/workplace/351545/great-resignation-really-great-discontent.aspx.

38. Medina, Elizabeth. "Job Satisfaction and Employee Turnover Intention: What Does Organizational Culture Have To Do With It?," Columbia University, 2012.

39. Dweck, Carol S. *Mindset*. London: Robinson, 2017.

40. Kar, Kamal, and Robert Chambers. "Handbook on Community-Led Total Sanitation." *Institute of Development Studies*, University of Sussex, 2008. https://doi.org/10.3362/9781780449753.000.

41. Kahneman, Daniel. *Thinking, Fast and Slow*. Farrar, Straus and Giroux, 2011.

42. George, Bill. *Authentic Leadership: Rediscovering the Secrets to Creating Lasting Value*. Prince Frederick, MD: Recorded Books, 2004.

43. Bar-On, Reuven. "Exploring the Neurological Substrate of Emotional and Social Intelligence." *The BarOn Model of Social and Emotional Intelligence* University of Texas Medical Branch (2006): 13–25. https://doi.org/10.1093/brain/awg177.

44. Eurich, Tasha. *Insight: How to Succeed by Seeing Yourself Clearly*. London: Pan Books, 2018.

45. Anderson, Terry D., Howard L. Shenson, and Ken Keis. *Entrepreneurial Style and Success Indicator*. Abbotsford, BC: Consulting Resource Group International, 2006.

46. *Emotional Intelligence 2.0* #1 Selling Emotional Intelligence Book. TalentSmartEQ, June 25, 2022. https://www.talentsmarteq.com/emotional-intelligence-2-0/.

47. Square Wheels® are a registered trademark of Performance Management Company, © Performance Management Company, 1993-2022. http://www.squarewheels.com/.

48. Crabtree, Steve. "Worldwide, 13% of Employees Are Engaged at Work." Gallup, February 23, 2022. https://news.gallup.com/poll/165269/worldwide-employees-engaged-work.aspx.

49. "To View Data Tables Click on One of the Links Below." U.S. Bureau of Labor Statistics, February 16, 2022. https://www.bls.gov/bdm/bdmage.htm.

50. Grant, Adam. *Think Again: The Power of Knowing What You Don't Know*. New York, NY: Random House Large Print, 2021.

Acknowledgments

I'd like to dedicate the lion's share of these acknowledgments to those who primarily operate in the background. Their work is essential to bringing a book to life and taking an author's writing to the next level. Books wouldn't be such a joy to read without their passion and dedication.

It's often them who turn a good story into an even more cohesive and enjoyable read. When they do a perfect job, their work goes unnoticed to the reader. Only when you read a book that didn't get enough attention from them, will you notice. That's when a book lacks flow, conciseness, or practical examples.

I am talking about the editors. With a keen eye, they make every book better. They spot logical breaks, unnecessary content, twists or turns, and holes in a story. They make it seem so effortless how they change a formulation—and suddenly the text reads and feels so much better than before.

I want to express my gratitude and respect to Rystana Petrovsky. She helped shape chapters that each feel like a full meal. I want to thank her for the relentless support, the fun we had editing, and for going above and beyond in her commitment to this book. We couldn't have done it without her—Rystana, thank you from the bottom of my heart for the great work you contributed to this project.

Jennie Wright contributed most notably through her writing and editing work, marketing genius, and a vision beyond the book. I value our collaboration and thank her for being a sounding board, helping me make sense of ideas others would simply consider crazy.

My agent, Sam Hiyate of The Rights Factory, shared his wealth of knowledge to help me bring this book to life. I'd like to thank him for all the resources he provided and the doors he opened for me. Having him as a sparring partner and consultant helped get this project started—and finished. May this be only the beginning of a long and successful collaboration.

Thanks to everyone at Wiley for believing in the idea of this book and making it become a reality, particularly Michelle Hacker and Zachary Schisgal.

Every one of you who shared the book with friends, colleagues, networks, and platforms—thanks for spreading the word and thereby helping others become *Next-Level Entrepreneurs*.

Finally, nine guest authors contributed to this anthology. Thank you for offering your unique perspectives and experiences. Hermann Simon, Sheetal Khullar, Charlene Li, Terry Jackson, Angela Howard, Jerry Fu, Tony Martignetti, Teresa Quinlan, and Ken Keis. I'm grateful to have met every single one of you. Your work and personalities enrich my life. It is a pleasure holding this book; seeing my work alongside yours fills me with joy and pride. We did this together. Danke.

About the Author

Alex Brueckmann is a strategy practitioner with over 20 years of business experience. He is the author of *The Strategy Legacy* (2023), which is based on his consulting work around the globe. His clients include start-ups, executive teams, and CEOs looking to achieve greater strategic clarity. He's been praised for his honest ways of bringing actionable strategy advice to entrepreneurs and executives.

An entrepreneur himself, Alex built and scaled businesses in Europe and North America. For the varying needs of his clients, he offers a range of online courses, workshops, and consulting packages.

Alex holds a B.Sc. in General Management from European Business School (EBS) in Germany, as well as certifications from Harvard Business School and INSEAD.

He lives in Vancouver with his wife and son.

Also available by Alex Brueckmann:
The Strategy Legacy (Summer 2023)

*T*he Strategy Legacy is perfect for leaders, practitioners, and entrepreneurs who want to shape the future of their businesses, without relying on external consultants. Alex Brueckmann demonstrates actionable solutions readers can put into practice right away, including a proven eight-step process for leading strategy design and implementation.

This book is a rare find – Brueckmann brings clarity to often fuzzy concepts behind business strategy, to properly define organizational identity. The author addresses strategy by going beyond how we normally think of it, linking culture and identity to make strategy more personal, and a more noble cause. *The Strategy Legacy* is an indispensable guide to shaping profitable businesses that positively impact employees, shareholders, society, and the planet.

The author vividly illustrates pitfalls to avoid, while setting inspiring examples to follow, embedded in the Nine Elements of Organizational Identity. This tried and tested framework aligns high-performing organizations around key aspects of their existence: people-centric, purpose-driven, and values-based, anchored in capability building, and management systems.

Alex Brueckmann writes with intelligence, passion, and humor. He weaves his corporate experience and consulting expertise to stitch together the core facets of successful businesses. The book is full of resources and techniques that everyone can pick up and put to work.

The Strategy Legacy will be available in Summer 2023.